Majorca
Island in the Sun
2nd Edition

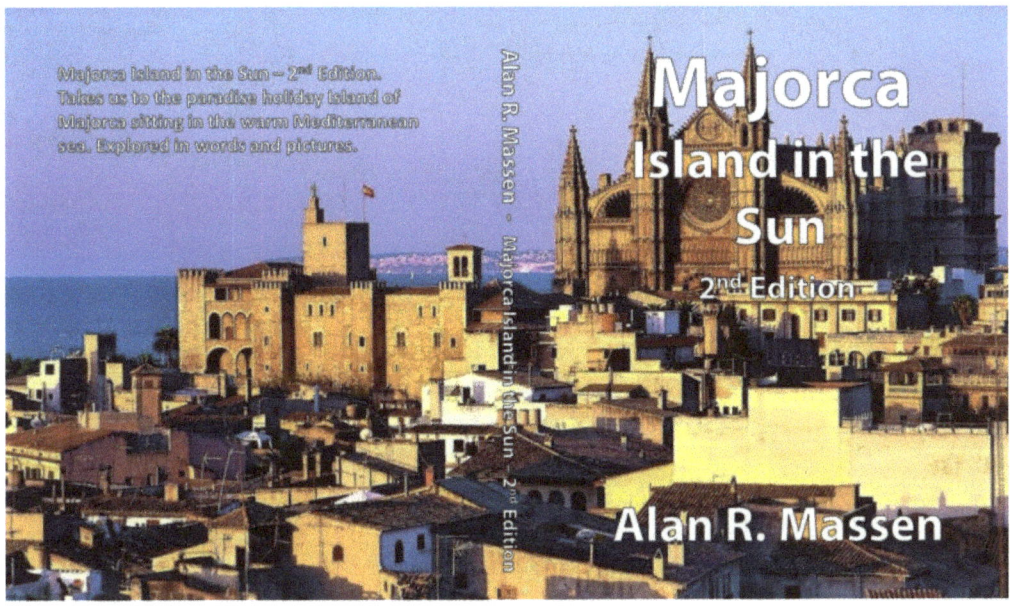

Majorca Island in the Sun focuses on the paradise Spanish holiday island of Majorca in the warm Mediterranean blue azure sea explored in words and pictures by Norfolk watercolour artist Alan R. Massen. Susie and I have holidayed on the island in the past and it really is a journey into the sun.

by Norfolk watercolour artist - Alan R. Massen
Published in Great Britain by Rainbow Publications UK

First Published in 2016 by Rainbow Publications UK
2nd Edition Published in 2019 by Rainbow Publications UK
Copyright © 2019 Alan R. Massen

The moral right of Alan R. Massen to be identified as the author of this work has been asserted in accordance with the UK Copyright, Designs and Patents Act of 1988. All rights reserved.

No part of this book may be reproduced, or stored in a retrieval system, or transmitted in any form or by any means, electronic, mechanical, photocopying, recording, or otherwise, without the prior written permission of both the author and the above publisher of this book All imagery and illustrations

© Alan R. Massen

Neither the publisher nor the author can accept liability for the use of any of the materials, methods or information recommended in this book or for any consequences arising out of their use, nor can they be held responsible for any errors or omissions that may be found in the text or may occur at a future date as a result of changes in rules, laws or equipment All manufacturers, sellers, product names and services identified in this book are used in editorial fashion and for the benefit of such companies with no intention of any infringement of trademarks. No such use or the use of any trade name is intended to convey endorsement or other affiliation with this book

Paperback Edition ISBN 978-0-9933962-7-4
Typeset in Minion Pro
Published in Great Britain by Rainbow Publications UK

About the Author

Alan was born in the city of Norwich in the county of Norfolk, England in November 1949. When Alan was still a teenager he started painting whilst attending art classes in Norwich. In his mid-teens he had two paintings accepted for a National Art Exhibition held in London and other major UK cities. Alan spent most of his working life as a professional Health and Safety Advisor and rarely picked up a paint brush until he, his wife Susie and daughter Ginny (his other daughter Mandy is married and lives with her husband Adrian in Sheffield) moved out of the city of Norwich into the countryside in 1993. They moved to a little village called East Lexham in the heart of Norfolk. The village was very peaceful and pretty. This helped inspire Alan to take up watercolour painting once again.

In 2004 they moved to another small West Norfolk village near Downham Market where they still live today. In 2008 Alan had to retire due to ill health (bad knees) and whilst he still painted regularly he began to spend more and more time gardening. In 2013 his wife Susie suggested that he kept a gardening diary to record his adventures in the garden and capture the changing seasons, animals, birds and the successes and failures of being a gardener he encountered.

By the following year Susie suggested that he should write a book from his diary and include illustrations of both the garden and his artwork. In 2014 Alan's first book was published by Creative Gateway called **"Retiring to the Garden – Year One"**. This proved such a success that Alan decided to follow this up with his second book called **"Retiring into a Rainbow"** featuring his watercolour paintings. He then in 2015 published **"Retiring to Our Garden – Year Two"** published this time by Rainbow Publications UK. He then re-issued his first two books this time in a **"Second Edition"**. Also published by Rainbow Publications UK.

His next planned publications are: **"Skiathos a Greek Island Paradise"** and **"Norfolk the County of my Birth"**, **"Art Inspired by a Rainbow"**. He has recently completed four new books which are entitled **"Majorca Island in the Sun"**, **"Ibiza Island of Dreams"**, **"Flip-flops and Shades on Thassos"** and finally **"Mardle and a Troshin' in Norfolk"** and these will be published by Rainbow Publications UK in the near future.

I hope you will enjoy visiting the Sunshine Island of Majorca with me…

Book by the same Author
Retiring to the Garden – Year 1

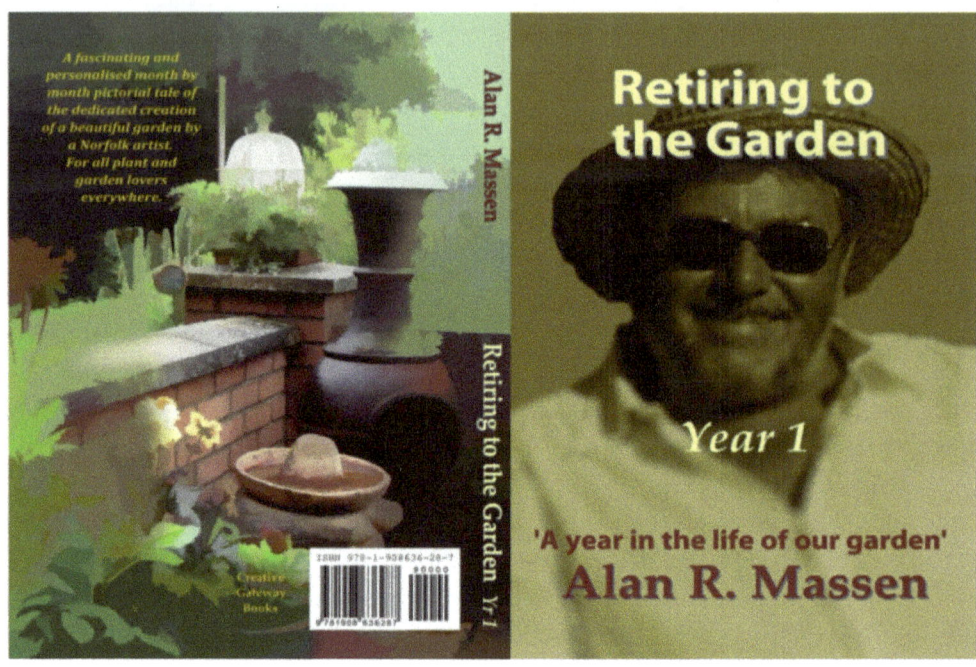

A fascinating and personalised month by month pictorial tale of the dedicated creation of a beautiful garden by Norfolk Watercolour Artist Alan R. Massen.

For all plant lovers everywhere…
Published in Great Britain by Creative Gateway

Book by the same Author

Retiring into a Rainbow - 2nd Edition

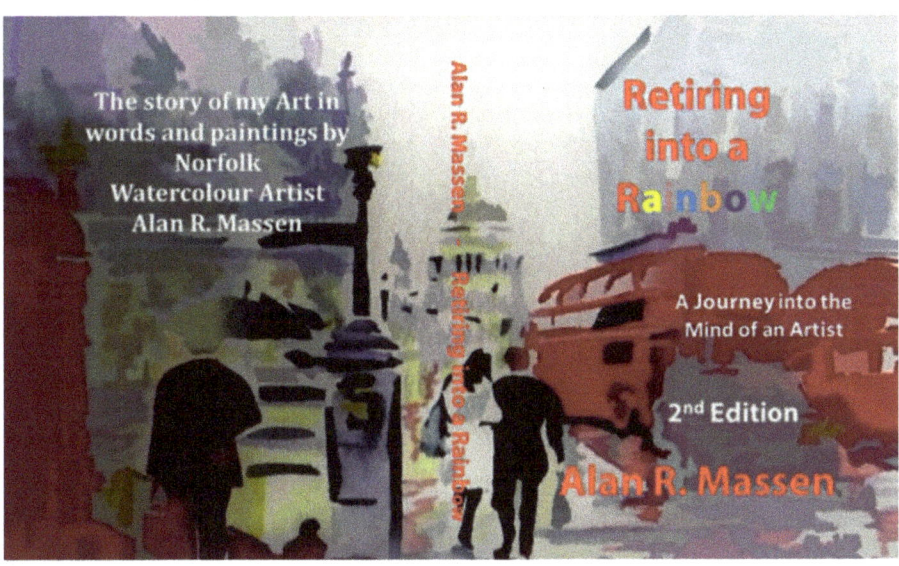

This beautifully illustrated book will take you through an incredible journey into the mind of Norfolk watercolour artist Alan R. Massen as he describes the inspiration, background and emotional meaning behind a large selection of his paintings, created over a period of more than twenty years…

Published 1st Edition by Creative Gateway and 2nd Edition by Rainbow Publications UK

Book by the same Author

Retiring to Our Garden – Year Two

The continuation of the fascinating and personalised month by month pictorial tale of the dedicated creation of a beautiful garden which is now in its second year by Norfolk Watercolour Artist Alan R. Massen.

This is a must for all plant lovers everywhere.
Published by Rainbow Publications UK

Book by the same Author
Retiring to Our Garden – Year One
2nd Edition

A fascinating and personalised month by month pictorial tale of the dedicated creation of a beautiful garden by Norfolk Watercolour Artist Alan R. Massen.

For all plant lovers everywhere…

Published 1st Edition by Creative Gateway and 2nd Edition by Rainbow Publications UK

Book by the same Author
Skiathos a Greek Island Paradise

This beautifully illustrated book by Norfolk Watercolour Artist Alan R. Massen will take you through an incredible journey to the beautiful Greek Island of Skiathos which is the best known of the Sporades Islands. People are drawn by the allure of its beaches along with pretty villages, pine covered hills and a perfect climate.

This is Alan and Susie's idea of paradise…

Published in Great Britain by Rainbow Publications UK

Book by the same Author

Norfolk the County of my Birth

A celebration of the County of the authors birth in which Norfolk Watercolour Artist Alan R. Massen takes the reader on an artwork journey around Norfolk.

Published in Great Britain by Rainbow Publications UK

Book by the same Author

Art Inspired by a Rainbow

In 2016, Alan R. Massen, the Norfolk watercolour artist, decided to produce this book which he hopes will take the reader on a pictorial journey using some of his favourite paintings and artworks. He believes that every picture tells a story and by using all the colours of the rainbow he hopes that the reader will be inspired to imagine the story behind each painting…

by Norfolk Watercolour Artist Alan R. Massen
Published in Great Britain by Rainbow Publications UK

Book by the same Author

Majorca Island in the Sun

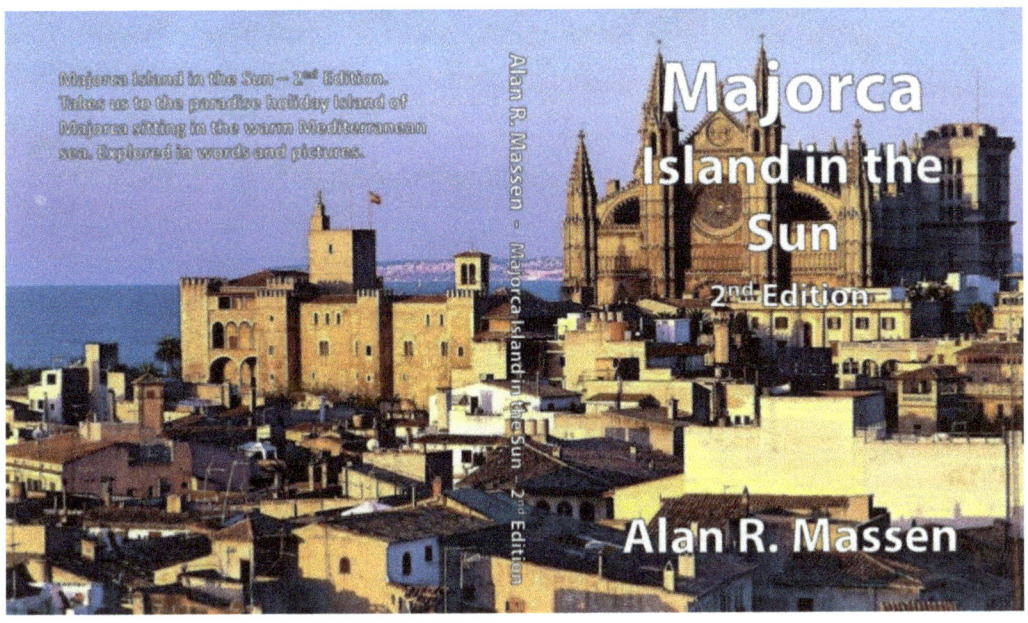

Majorca Island in the Sun focuses on the paradise Spanish holiday island of Majorca in the warm Mediterranean blue azure sea explored in words and artwork pictures by Norfolk watercolour artist Alan R. Massen. We have holidayed on the island in the past and it really is a journey into the sunshine.

"A journey into the Sunshine"

Published in Great Britain by Rainbow Publications UK

Book by the same Author

Ibiza Island of Dreams

Ibiza Island of Dreams focuses on the paradise Spanish holiday island of Ibiza in the warm Mediterranean blue azure sea explored in words and artwork pictures by Norfolk watercolour artist Alan R. Massen. We have holidayed on the island in the past and it really is a journey into the sunshine.

Published in Great Britain by Rainbow Publications UK

Book by the same Author

Flip-flops and Shades on Thassos

The paradise Greek holiday island of Thassos in the warm Mediterranean blue azure sea explored in words and artwork pictures

"A journey into the Sunshine"

by Norfolk Watercolour Artist Alan R. Massen
Published in Great Britain by Rainbow Publications UK

Book by the same Author

Mardle and a Troshin' in Norfolk

A Journey through ten months in my life in Norfolk in 2015 - 2016 explored in words and artwork pictures. "An old Norfolk boys ramblings".

by Norfolk Watercolour Artist Alan R. Massen
Published in Great Britain by Rainbow Publications UK

Dedication

I would like to dedicate this book to my football team Norwich City FC (the Canaries of Carrow Road, Norwich) who I have been supporting for more than sixty years. On Saturday 27th April 2019 Norwich City beat Blackburn Rovers 2 - 1 at home to gain promotion back to the Premier League next season. In November 2019 I will be seventy years of age and I am so proud and excited that my team will be playing, against the big boys, once more in the top division of English football league. On the Ball City - Come on you YELLOWS…

The team, club badge, my canaries watercolour and Alan proudly wearing his Yellow and Green

I hope you will enjoy my latest book on the Spanish paradise Island of Majorca…

Contents

Introduction …………………………………..	1
Majorca: History, Climate and Geography ..	7
Facts About Majorca ……………………..	14
Out and About on Majorca………………..	20
Exploring Majorca ……………………..	28
Palma de Mallorca ………………………	190
Leaving Majorca ………..……………….	198
Acknowledgement ……………………..	202

Copyright © 2019 Alan R. Massen

Introduction

Introduction: Majorca Island in the Sun

Majorca is the largest island in the Balearics and it may make you think of beach resorts and holidays, but there are plenty of other ways to enjoy both its coastline and the interior of the island. It is a good idea to visit, particularly in autumn and winter when the crowds have gone and the temperature is more suitable for outdoor activities. Susie and I have holidayed on Majorca several times in the past. During our summer two weeks holidays to the sunshine island of Majorca we have stayed in the resorts of Porto Colom, Magaluf, Porto de Pollenca, S'illot and Sa Coma and have always enjoyed our stays and had a great time. The beaches are lovely, the seawater clear, blue and warm. This really is a beautiful island packed with things to do and places to go or you can just soak up the sun and enjoy a good book, swim or have a long cold drink. One thing you must do during any stay on the island is to spend some time in the capitol Palma de Majorca were you can have a cold drink and watch a cricket match on the central green of the capital. Another must do is to take the islands train to Soller and sample the fresh grown oranges. Also try and visit as many of the lovely beach resorts and villages that are all the way around the island...

Introduction: When to go

Although the beach holiday season gets going in May and winds down in October, the island is beautiful in early spring when the almond blossom is out. It is therefore, well worth a visit in spring.

The hottest months of the summer season are July and August, all the Balearics are good for activity holidays, whether easy or more challenging; with plenty of wild life to see on the island if you are interested in plants, animals or birds…

Introduction: When to go

From late January and throughout February, the almond trees and there are about four million of them are in flower in the valleys and across the plains of Majorca.

Above we see nectarine and almond blossom on Majorca in the spring when on the island it is traditionally low season, when accommodation and flights are cheapest, and while it may not be warm enough to lie on the beach, the temperature is usually just right for exploring the countryside in the sunshine and seeing all the lovely flowers and animals of the island…

Introduction: Laws and etiquette

Above we see a view of Palma cathedral from the seaward side. This is truly a wonderful and beautiful building and a must see for any visitor to the island.

Some of the things you need to know: Remember to take a couple of photocopies of your European Health Insurance Card and passport, as you will need them for any medical treatment. You must carry your passport with you by law. You sometimes have to show your passport when paying by debit or credit card. If driving, you must have two warning triangles, two reflective bibs, a spare tyre and spare headlamp bulbs. Children under 12 are only allowed in the front seat fitted with approved safety belts…

Introduction: Laws and etiquette

On Majorca it is not usual to share tables, even in fast-food joints. Anyone you are introduced to by friends will want to kiss you on both cheeks, but this does not apply to hotel staff. This is the local way of doing things so do not worry it is common to see people greeting one another with hugs and kisses.

On Majorca it is usual for the local inhabitants to have their lunch from 2 pm, dinner from 9 pm at the very earliest, though 10 pm is the norm. In resorts, however, you can usually eat any time you like. So if like us you like to eat your lunch at about 12.30 pm and your evening meal at about 8 pm then you can. This has the added advantage of the restaurants being quieter and will have plenty of seating with the best views available…

Introduction: Laws and etiquette

One thing that is worth knowing for the visitor is that most bars will not mind if you go in just to use the toilets. Although they certainly would like you to have a drink while you are there. It is rare to see Spaniards rolling drunk in public. It is a bit cheaper to have drinks or tapas at the bar rather than sitting at a table, and sitting outside will usually cost a little extra. Locals usually leave very small tips such as just odd change for drinks and snacks, and often nothing at all. A 10 per cent tip for a meal is considered generous and five per cent is more the norm unless you are somewhere really upmarket, when international rules come into play. If breakfast is not included in your hotel rate, it is much cheaper and more fun to go to a local bar for your morning meal…

History, Climate and Geography

The History of Majorca:

Evidence of Paleolithic habitation has been found on Mallorca, from 6000-4000 BC. In 123 BC the island was under Roman occupation, and during this time it flourished. In 534 AD it was overturned by the Byzantine Empire and under their rule Christianity flourished. In 902 AD the Moors conquered Mallorca and improved much of the island's economy, through agriculture and developing local industries. They stayed for nearly two centuries until the Catalans finally overturned their rule. The official language is Catalan, but secondary is Castilian…

The History of Majorca:

Mallorca's, or as we British like to call it Majorca, inclusive holiday tourism started in the early 1960's and they are still ahead of the game with ideas and improvements. Palma airport, seen above, has increased in size over the years to accommodate all the extra people who have made this island their island of choice for their summer holidays. Mistakes that were made in the sixties or seventies have been rectified with many of the resorts tidied up and unwanted high rise hotels demolished to make green areas and make the island more attractive to the visitor…

The Climate of Majorca:

Majorca (Mallorca) enjoys a typical Mediterranean climate, with mild winters and hot summers. During the months of July and August, the weather is hot and beautifully sunny, boasting around 11 hours of sun daily. During the winter, the weather can get chilly, but generally you can enjoy fine, mild weather on most days of the year…

The Geography of Majorca:

Majorca has two mountainous regions called the Serra de Tramuntana and Serres de Llevant and locals and visitors alike enjoy there wonderful views and wild life all year round.

The ranges are about 70 km (43 miles) in length and occupy the north-western and eastern thirds of the island. The highest peak on Majorca is Puig Major at 1,445 m (4,741 feet) in the Serra de Tramuntana…

The Geography of Majorca:

The northeast coast of Majorca comprises of two bays: the Badia de Pollença and the larger Badia d'Alcúdia. We have holidayed in both these resorts in the past. The northern coast is rugged and has many cliffs. The central zone extending from Palma is generally a flat and fertile plain known as Es Pla.

The island has a variety of caves both above and below sea-level. Two of the caves above sea-level also contain underground lakes and are open to the public for tours. Both are near the eastern coastal town of Porto Cristo, the caves dels Hams and the caves del Drach. Susie, Ginny and I went to the resort and visited the caves during our last visit to the island…

The Geography of Majorca:

Majorca is the largest by area and second most populated island of Spain (after Tenerife in the Canary Islands).

There are two small islands off the coast of Majorca. They are called Cabrera, southeast of Palma and Dragonera west of Palma…

The Geography of Majorca:

Majorca has a long history of seafaring. Majorcan cosmographies and cartographers developed breakthroughs in cartographic techniques, namely the "normal portolan chart", which was fine-tuned for navigational use and the plotting by compass of navigational routes, prerequisites for the discovery of the New World…

Facts About Majorca

Mallorca (in English also called Majorca) is arguably the best known and largest of the Balearic Islands in the Mediterranean.

Majorca is a very beautiful island with stunning scenery. There are wooded hillsides, towering mountains, gentle valleys, olive groves, ancient towns and villages, sheltered bays and marvellous sandy beaches. In other words Majorca has it all…

Facts about Majorca:

It is said by many that Mallorca is a truly upmarket holiday destination, with plenty to see. So why not come and see for yourself.

Since the 1950's Majorca has become a major tourist destination, and the tourism business has become the main source of revenue for the island. The island received millions of tourists, and the boom in the tourism industry has provided significant growth in the economy of the country…

Facts about Majorca:

The members of the Spanish Royal Family spend their summer holidays on Majorca where the Marivent Palace is located. The Marivent Palace is the royal family's summer residence and is under the care of the government of the Balearic Islands. So you will be in very good company if you holiday on this island…

Facts about Majorca:

There are more than 2,400 restaurants on the island of Majorca, ranging from small bars to high end restaurants. So it will be easy for you to find an eating establishment during your stay on the island.

Olives (see above) and almonds are typical of the Majorcan diet. Among the food items that are typically Majorcan are saffron rice cooked with chicken, pork and vegetables, and the sweet pastry ensaïmada (see above). Herbs de Majorca is an herbal liqueur and worth a try when you are sitting comfortably in a bar…

Facts about Majorca:

The popularity of Majorca island as a tourist destination has been steadily growing since the 1950's, with many artists and academics choosing to visit and/or live on the island.

Visitors to Majorca continued to increase with holiday makers in the 1970's approaching 3 million a year. In 2010 over 6 million visitors came to Majorca staying at the many resorts. In 2013, Majorca was visited by nearly 9.5 million tourists, and the Balearic Islands as a whole reached 13 million tourists…

Facts about Majorca:

The island has thousands of rooms available for rent which means that Majorca's economy is largely dependent on its tourism industry. Holiday makers are attracted to the island by the large number of sandy beaches, warm weather, good shopping, outdoor markets and high-quality tourist amenities…

Out and About on Majorca

On Majorca professional cyclists come to train in the Serra de Tramuntana mountain range in the west of the island, which is now a World Heritage Site. If that sounds a bit challenging, base yourself in the foothills of the range in the Es Raigeur area. Or stick to the reassuringly flat Es Pla in the centre of the island, where rural tourism is also quietly gaining ground…

Out and About on Majorca:

Although not untouched by tourism, the hitherto unfashionable towns and villages of the interior of Majorca have hung onto their traditions and are now coming into their own to visit or even stay in.

A day's cycling or hiking may well also involve visiting a winery, an olive mill or a farm to learn how sobrasada (see above), the Majorcan pork sausage, is made…

Out and About on Majorca:

On Majorca the chefs are reviving traditional recipes and adapting them to suit modern tastes both in the capital Palma, beach resorts and the towns and villages inland.

The cathedral in Palma de Mallorca (seen above) should be on everyone's agenda to visit whilst on the island. It should also be noted that there are now seven Michelin-starred restaurants on the island, serving dishes you are unlikely to find anywhere else in the world…

Out and About on Majorca:

On Majorca this renewed enthusiasm for the local cuisine is however also evident everywhere from unpretentious restaurants in mountain villages to the chic gastro bars and delis popping up in Palma.

If you can't get to see the almond blossom in early spring, go in late spring when the cherry trees are flowering, or in the autumn to witness or take part in the grape and olive harvests. Then head to a hidden cove along the coast to walk on the sandy beach and plunge into the turquoise seawater…

Out and About on Majorca:

Although on Majorca most resorts close down in the winter months, Palma is great for a weekend break all year round and life goes on in the villages. If you want to do more than just lie on a beach, take advantage of the low rates in winter and get a taste of the real life on the paradise island that is in the Balearics called Majorca. Palma Cathedral is also open all the year round…

Out and About on Majorca:

In the summer months, you might not want to move to far away from the beach whether that means snorkelling in a tiny rocky cove or sunbathing at one of the beach resorts. But there is always something to explore on Majorca, from honey-coloured villages to wildlife nature reserves. You should try and find the time to visit some of them whilst you are on the island…

Out and About on Majorca:

Getting around is easy by car or bus on Majorca and there are some wonderful walking and cycling routes. Spend at least a couple of days seeing the magnificent architecture and museums in Palma itself but remembering to leave plenty of time for shopping…

Out and About on Majorca:

Throughout Spain, local prefixes must be used when making phone calls. You have to dial the 971 Balearics prefix wherever you are on the island.

British consulate: Carrer Convent dels Caputxins 4, Edificio Orisba B 4ºD, Palma; 902 109356 (from Majorca or elsewhere in Spain); 00 34 917 146 300

Tourist office Palma: Casal Solleric, Passeig des Born 27 (971 729604); Parc de las Estacions (902 102 365) and Plaça de la Reina 2 (00 34 971 173 990).

Emergency services: dial 112

Currency: Euro.

Time difference: One hour ahead of UK.

Flight time: Majorca is approximately two and a half hours from the UK…

Exploring Majorca

When holidaying on Majorca rather than laying on a beach, one idea could be to spend a week exploring the Serra de Tramuntana on foot or by bike. This mountain range, running down the west of Majorca, has been made a World Heritage Site in recognition of the extraordinary techniques used to develop agriculture on its steep slopes over the centuries.

Or you could visit a few of the wineries in the centre of the island, or see the olive plantations or visit a village where local traditions are as strong as ever…

Exploring Majorca

It does not matter if you have been to the island of Majorca several times, there is always more to discover, particularly as there are now a stunning selection of rural hotels that provide a luxurious base for a week or two spent exploring the lush countryside in the interior of Majorca as well as its dramatic coastline…

Alaró

Alaró is a small, traditional town that is situated inland, surrounded by countryside and stunning mountain scenery. It is a taste of the real Majorca, the town is perfect for visitors seeking a restful holiday away from the main tourist resorts.

Alaró is situated about 30 km (about 19 miles) from Palma International Airport and has a short transfer time of around 20-40 minutes. Set in a remote, peaceful valley at the foot of the Sierra Tramuntana mountain range, the town is favoured for its remote and picturesque location. Packed with rustic buildings and winding, narrow cobbled streets, Alaró has a relaxed pace, and its location makes it a haven for cyclists, ramblers, hikers and casual walkers alike…

Alaró

Alaró has a charming town square, around which most of the action happens, with a selection of traditional bars and restaurants, shops and hotels. The town's church is also here. Around the square you can sit outside beneath parasols to soak up the ambience with a cold drink or two, or dine al fresco at one of the bar-cafes or restaurants in the square. You will find the town has a marked contrast to the tourist resorts on the coast. There is a small market on Saturday mornings, where you can buy all kinds of local produce such as lovely fresh fruit and vegetables, plus gifts, handmade jewellery, home wares and clothing. Alaró has several good bakeries selling delicious fresh bread and pastries. There is also a good butchers and a supermarket.

Romantic and pretty, Alaró has plenty of pulling power, with fabulous lush green countryside all around…

Alaró

The area is officially designated as a nature area of special interest no doubt due to its wealth of pine forests, olive trees, almond trees, a river, and great vistas of plains stretching away into the far distance.

In the area surrounding the plains rise two impressive mountains to dominate the skyline: Mount Alaró, the highest at 825 m (about 2,700 ft), and Mount S'Alcadena (about 813 m or 2,667 ft)…

Alaró

The most famous tourist attraction in Alaró is probably the castle (Castell d' Alaró), perched on top of a rocky mountainous outcrop called Puig Des Castell (Puig d' Alaró). Alaró Castle is situated on top of the mountain at over 800 ft above sea level, and so has a steep but enjoyable walk up to reach the top via an old stone road. When you get to the top of Puig Des Castell you are rewarded by breath-taking views over the countryside and beyond to the coast at Palma and Alcudia.

The views of Serra de Tramuntana mountain range are also impressive. The castle and battlements are steeped in history and there are numerous local legends based upon it. Alaró has a friendly, relaxed atmosphere and will leave you in no doubt that this is the real deal when it comes to authentic Majorca…

Alaró

When staying or visiting the village remember to kick back and enjoy the gentle pace of day to day life with siestas, tapas and alfresco dining.

A romantic and secluded town, Alaró nestles in gorgeous Majorcan countryside, with spectacular views, wild flowers and has plenty of charm....

Alcudia

Alcudia is a large town in north east Majorca, with plenty of history and sights, just inland from the port area of Puerto Alcudia. For a taste of the real Majorca, consider Alcudia for your next holiday in the sun.

This ancient town is steeped in history and packed with relics of its colourful past. With narrow, winding streets lined with beautiful little houses and buildings, the town offers a sample of traditional Mallorcan life, and a chance to discover a fascinating and historically important town, some parts of which date as far back as the 14th century…

Alcudia

Like many of Majorca's towns, Alcudia was built a couple of miles inland from the port area. Alcudia has old defensive walls and gates that surround the town that were to protect the main town and its residents from invaders who might arrive by sea. In Alcudia the port area known as Puerto Alcudia is a thriving holiday resort in its own right, with a lovely beach and marina and a number of hotels, bars and restaurants. Puerto Alcudia is often confusingly referred to simply as Alcudia but the old town is quite separate. Being slightly off the beaten track, the old town tends to attract visitors seeking history and culture.

This pretty, ancient town is packed with historical significance and the site has Phoenician and Moorish influences which date as far back as the 7th century BC. Visitors can take advantage of guided walking tours for more detailed information about Alcudia's turbulent history…

Alcudia

One of the main attractions of Alcudia is the historical significance of the town in Roman times and examples of Roman buildings can be seen throughout the town.

Alcudia was once the capital of Mallorca, and the town features in many significant events of Majorca's past. Close to the town can be viewed the ruins of an old Roman town and a fascinating amphitheatre…

Alcudia

The area is great for walking holidays and exploring the north of the island. There is some spectacular scenery around this area, with the northern part of the Serra Tramuntera mountain range just to the west, and plenty of hills and peaks providing wonderful viewpoints of the scenery all around. Alcudia is not a typical resort, the town is not sleepy and has a cosmopolitan atmosphere, and bustles with activity on Tuesday and Sunday mornings, when there is a street market. Head there for a bargain. If you need a little beach time, then a trip down to Puerto Alcudia is well worthwhile.

Set on the vast and impressive Alcudia Bay, a beautiful stretch of white, sandy beach that runs for over 10 km (6 miles), along the full length of the resort. There is also a very luxurious and pretty marina, around which you will find a great range of shops, restaurants and bars…

Alcudia

Alcudia is roughly 60 km (about 35 miles) from Palma International Airport, and typical transfer time from the airport to this area is around an hour to an hour and a half, depending on traffic.

"Alcudia is one of Majorca's most significant historic towns, with roots as far back as 7 BC, roman ruins and a surrounding stunning countryside to explore."…

Andratx

Un-spoilt Majorca at its best: Andratx is a charming old town in south-west Majorca, with winding, cobbled streets, a famous street market and fabulous views. Andratx is a quaint, traditional Mallorcan town in the south west of the island. Packed with narrow winding streets, the town offers a taste of the real Majorca, away from the main tourist trail. The town is about 35 km (about 22 miles) from Palma and the airport.

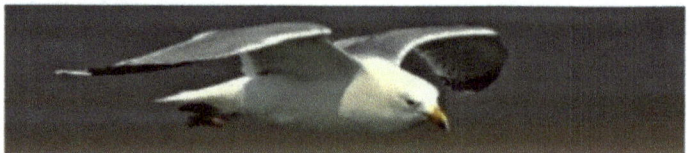

Like many coastal towns in Majorca, the town is set about 5 km (about 3 miles) inland from the port. The pace is relaxed and the vibe is quite cosmopolitan here. Andratx is off the beaten track as far as package holidays go, and the area is popular with countryside lovers and walkers. Surrounded by lush greenery, citrus and olive groves, almond trees and countryside dotted with traditional Mallorcan fincas, Andratx is perhaps more of a base for explorers than a typical holiday resort. This pretty little town is not particularly tourist-orientated, and is not really featured by any major tour operators. However, Andratx is popular with foreigners who own second homes here, and the town has many impressive private homes and villas, and its beauty and relatively secluded location has been attracting the rich and famous for decades…

Andratx

Andratx has some great restaurants and bars, and is home to a large renowned market, held weekly on Wednesdays selling fresh local produce. For art lovers, there is a large private art gallery which has a large collection of contemporary art to enjoy…

Andratx

Visitors to Andratx town will appreciate the stunning views over Puerto Andratx and beyond. The port area still has working fishing boats bobbing about that bring home their catch each evening. The old town of Andratx is very pretty and retains many traditional features. It is Split into two districts, Pantaleu and Pou Amunt, the higher end has traditional shuttered town houses and narrow, stepped, cobbled streets leading to traditional town squares.

There is a very impressive 13th century church (Santa Maria) at the top of the hill, from where you can enjoy magnificent sweeping views back down over the town to the port area and beyond to the sea. Andratx was once protected by walls, protecting the town from pirate attacks, and you can still see remnants of the old wall today. Protection from invaders is also the reason why Andratx town, like many others in Majorca, was built a couple of miles inland. The So Na Gaiana's tower was used to protect the town from pirate raids…

Andratx

The town of Andratx has an important place in Mallorcan culture and history, having been a major town and home to several prominent figures in Mallorcan history, including King Jaime I and the Bishop of Barcelona back in the 13th century.

As there is only one very tiny beach (in Puerto Andratx), this is not a place that attracts beach-lovers. It is an ideal base for anyone wishing to explore the area, which has some stunning countryside, some wind turbines and walking trails…

Andratx

Transfer time from the airport to Andratx is typically about half an hour or so.

For the authentic Mallorca, look no further than the traditional old town of Andratx, with cobbled streets, old town houses and amazing views…

Caimari

The village is a tranquil and picturesque and charming Majorcan village set deep in the countryside. Caimari is just the ticket if you're looking for a peaceful and relaxing holiday in the sun.

Set inland, at the edge of the Serra de Tramuntana mountain range, Caimari is a taste of rural Majorca and is sleepy, laid back and picturesque…

Caimari

Caimari is within the municipality of Selva, located about 30 km (19 miles) from Palma airport. The village is just north of Inca, and transfer time is typically around 40 minutes. Not the usual run-of-the-mill holiday resort. Caimari is a traditional Mallorcan village, with plenty of historic and cultural interest. Visitors wishing to explore Majorca's natural history as well as walkers, ramblers and cyclists will find Caimari a great base for exploring the countryside.

The village of Caimari itself is a delightful and ancient site, with winding narrow streets and a typically Majorcan village square, Plaza Mayor (Plaç a Major), which serves as the central focal point of the village. Around the charming plaza you will find a handful of cafes and a couple of restaurants where you can sit and enjoy a spot of people-watching over a cool drink or two and a bowl of olives...

Caimari

The shops are limited in the village but there are a couple, including a bakery. There is also a 19th century church in the square. Its bell still tolls every quarter of an hour.

There is little in the way of tourist attractions in Caimari, so it's a destination that is ideal for holiday makers seeking peace and relaxation…

Caimari

The pace here is laid-back and offers spectacular views, lush countryside and a friendly, authentic Majorcan welcome. You will feel as though you have gone back in time when you visit Caimari. The pace of change here is, fortunately, slow, and the village retains an air of tradition and Majorcan culture.

Historically, Caimari's trade has been in leather and olive oil, and as well as a working olive press in the centre of the village, you will find groves of olive, almond, lemon and orange trees. There is an annual olive fair held in Caimari in mid-November, for which the village is decorated with olive leaves and there are stalls selling olives and other local produce including fruit, vegetables and wine. The fair is quaint and simple, with demonstrations of the horse-driven olive press, pony rides for children and a very friendly atmosphere. There are plenty of tasting opportunities around the fair, which raises money for charities, and you can sample all kinds of olive oil and the local liqueur, hierbas…

Caimari

Its central location makes Caimari an ideal base for explorers in all directions. There are several good walking routes through the groves for an enchanting ramble. To the north and west, the Sierra Tramuntana mountain range with its stunning views and woodlands. To the north east, beaches at Puerto Alcudia and Puerto Pollensa, and the Cap de Formentor beyond.

If you want a little more action, the more energetic south coast resorts and city of Palma is within easy reach. You are spoiled for choice if you have access to a car. Closer to Caimari, the nearby village of Selva has a market on Thursdays. Caimari is a secluded, rustic village set inland amongst stunning countryside. It is authentic, rustic and relaxed....

Cala Bona

Cala Bona is a lovely family resort, retaining the charm of its origins as a traditional fishing village, yet offering plenty of facilities for holiday makers of all ages.

Like many of Majorca's popular resorts, Cala Bona was originally a traditional fishing village, and has transformed over the last few decades into a delightful family holiday resort…

Cala Bona

Situated on the east coast of Majorca, close to Cala Millor, the resort enjoys fabulous scenery and three gorgeous sandy beaches. Cala Bona is about 65 km (approximately 40 miles) from Palma Airport, and the journey over to this part of the east coast can take up to two hours.

Popular with British holiday makers, Cala Bona has plenty of attractions to keep everyone entertained, yet retains a traditional Spanish flavour, helped in part by the fact that it has retained a small working harbour. This also means that the seafood restaurants are amazing! Cala Bona has a friendly, welcoming atmosphere and it well suited to families. There are plenty of bars and restaurants of every variety. The promenade stretches to Cala Millor with shops and bars, or you can just enjoy the amazing views towards the Punta De'n Amer headland, which offers the visitor a remote and special viewpoint amongst Mallorcan flora, pines and craggy rocks…

Cala Bona

Cala Bona means "the good bay" and it certainly lives up to its name. Stretching for 2 km towards Cala Millor, the sand on each of the beaches is white and soft, and the sea is warm and crystal clear. The sand slopes gently into the sea here, so it's a great, safe place for families with young children. So get your bucket and spade for long happy days on the beach.

There are plenty of water sports facilities such as scuba diving, windsurfing, kitesurfing, sailing and fishing, and you can hire sunbeds and parasols on the beach. You can take trips on glass bottomed boats from Cala Bona, so you can enjoy views down into the sparkling clear seawater as well…

Cala Bona

If you enjoy exploring, Cala Bona has a few original narrow streets to explore, as well as the picturesque harbour area. There are also some protected areas of special environmental interest close by, for nature lovers.

If you want to explore a little further afield, it's possible to catch a bus from Cala Bona to Alcudia. If you have access to a car, you could take a day trip to Sa Coma, S'Illot or Porto Cristo. We have stayed in Sa Coma and S'illot in the past and enjoyed our stay in these resorts very much. Cala Bona is a charming beach resort on the east coast, with a working harbour and tourist facilities aplenty…

Cala d'Or

Cala d'Or is a charming and relaxed resort with several coved beaches, a marina, and a wealth of chic bars, restaurants, boutiques and shops. This is a great place to wonder around and take in the atmosphere.

The east coast resort of Cala d'Or is one of the prettiest on the island of Majorca. Located in the district of Santanyi, Cala d'Or is about 65 km (about 40 miles) from Palma airport…

Cala d'Or

Like many of Majorca's resorts, Cala d'Or has evolved from a small fishing village into a popular tourist resort, packed with bars, restaurants and shops. The resort retains its picturesque qualities and authentic Mallorcan charm. The resort has an upmarket, stylish feel, with a stunning marina in the centre, surrounded by cobbled streets, whitewashed low-rise buildings and villas. Set along seven sandy coves (calas) providing picture-postcard perfect beaches of soft, golden sand, the resort has a relaxed, sophisticated vibe that attracts the rich and famous. The stunning marina is set in the largest of Cala d'Or's coves, Cala Llonga. The remainder of the resort stretches out in both directions along the coast, around the other coves.

You can walk the full length of the resort, or take a ride on the tourist road train which will take you to all of the nearby coves…

Cala d'Or

All of the beaches in Cala d'Or are quite small, but perfectly formed, edged with pines trees, and offering stunning views. Perfect for sunbathing, swimming and family fun, the sheltered coves are real sun-traps, and have warm clear water, but be aware that they can all become quite crowded in peak season. So do not forget to take your suntan cream, sunglasses, a hat and a large towel with you.

Cala Gran and Cala Llonga are the largest beaches and have facilities for hiring sun loungers and parasols, as well as sailing, kite-surfing, windsurfing and scuba-diving. You can also hire pedaloes, go horse riding, take trips on glass-bottomed boats or hire a luxury yacht for the day. So there is plenty to do at Cala d'Or for all ages…

Cala d'Or

Cala d'Or has a pedestrian zone around the Cala Gran area, where you will find an array of bars, restaurants and shops selling all kinds of souvenirs, crafts, clothing and holiday accessories, inflatable's etc., plus designer boutiques for the more discerning shoppers. Evening entertainment in Cala d'Or is low-key and mainly hotel based, but you will find a good selection of livelier bars and a couple of discos around the pedestrian zone. Cala d'Or is not a party resort though, so may be best suited to families and those seeking peace and quiet. For eating out, you will find plenty of choice from traditional Spanish dining and high class seafood restaurants, to international cuisine, pizzas, fast food and pub grub, every taste is catered for.

On the whole, the quality of restaurants in Cala d'Or is very good, with plenty of high quality eateries. For a night to remember dine under the stars in one of the open air fish restaurants…

Cala d'Or

You will find plenty of hotels and holiday accommodation to suit your budget in Cala d'Or, with a few luxury five-star hotels in the resort and many villas and apartments.

From Cala d'Or you can visit markets at Felanitx on a Sunday (we went on both Sundays during one of our holidays and enjoyed the market and walking around the village). There is also a market at Santanyi on a Wednesday and a Saturday…

Cala d'Or

It is possible to catch buses to other east coast resorts, although the timetables may be somewhat unreliable. There is also a large market at Inca on Saturday mornings. There is also a bus to the city of Palma. Also within easy reach are the Caves of Drach (see below) where Susie, Ginny and I had a great day out.

Cala d'Or is a sophisticated and stylish resort, with a friendly and relaxed atmosphere. It is a picturesque and charming place to stay or visit. It is a place to relax and unwind, take in the views, and enjoy the warm sunny days. So relax and take in the views from picturesque Cala d'Or, one of Majorca's prettiest resorts, edged with sandy coves and with a charming marina in the centre…

Cala Mayor

Cala Mayor is a well-established family resort, close to the city of Palma, with a vast array of amenities for holiday makers of all ages.

Just 20 km (about 12 miles) from Palma International Airport, Cala Mayor is a lively coastal holiday resort in the municipal district of Calvia, in south west Majorca. Transfer time from the airport to Cala Mayor is 15 - 30 minutes, depending on the time of day and traffic…

Cala Mayor

Situated at the bottom of a hillside, along Cala Mayor Bay, a sweeping bay of golden sands tucked between rocky headlands, typical of many beach resorts in Majorca. An ideal place for families, the area has been catering for tourists for many decades, and was once one of the busiest and liveliest beach resorts on the island. Nowadays things have calmed down somewhat.

Alan in the sea…

Cala Mayor has been redeveloped and is considered slightly higher class than its neighbours Palma Nova and/or Magaluf. It offers modern facilities to suit most holiday makers. Cala Mayor has a small sandy beach, with fine sand and plenty of sun loungers and parasols for hire, plus toilet and shower facilities, lifeguards and first aid. The seawater is calm and clear and the beach has blue flag status. There are water sports facilities and boat trips available in the resort, as well as a sailing school…

Cala Mayor

In Cala Mayor and running alongside the beach is Avinguda de Joan Miro, a (quite busy) road that follows the coastline with a swathe of hotels, shops, bars and restaurants.

You can enjoy a pleasant stroll in the shade of palm trees as you browse the souvenir shops, and perhaps stop for refreshments along the way…

Cala Mayor

There are many hotels in the resort, and offers a wealth of choices for eating, drinking and shopping. There are plenty of good cafes and bars for refreshments, and lots of dining options. Seafood is very prominent and you will find lots of good fish restaurants, plus tapas and traditional Spanish and Majorcan food. There are also a selection of international restaurants and a few fast food places. Cala Mayor is close enough to Palma that it's a short taxi ride to the more sophisticated and lively city nightlife and trendy bars. There are spectacular views over to Palma Bay, and as far as Palma Nova to the south west.

As well as the amazing views, Cala Mayor has beach life, entertainment and fun. All the ingredients for a fabulous holiday in the sun. One bonus if you choose Cala Mayor for your holiday is its proximity to the city of Palma, which makes it a great base for anyone wanting to combine city sight-seeing and culture with the relaxation of a beach holiday. Yes you can have it all at Cala Mayor…

Cala Mayor

Regular buses run through Cala Mayor, so it's quite easy to get to Palma and around the south coast area, so you can easily explore neighbouring resorts like Illetas, Palma Nova or Magaluf. One year we stayed at Magaluf and used the buses to get between these resorts everyday.

Cala Mayor is also home to the Spanish royal family's official summer residence, Marivent Palace. Cala Mayor has all the ingredients for a holiday in the sun it has sandy beaches, hotels, bars and restaurants galore, and is close enough to Palma for city explorers…

Cala Millor

Cala Millor is a large, lively resort on the east coast of Majorca, within the district of Son Servera. Transfer times are typically around 2 hours, the resort being 65 km (about 40 miles) from Palma airport.

A modern resort, packed with tourist amenities, there is plenty going on in Cala Millor…

Cala Millor

The resort sprawls over some 6 km (about 4 miles) of beach within a sheltered bay, between rocky headlands. It enjoys fantastic views over the sea. The sandy beach at Cala Millor gently slopes into clear sparkling water, warmed by its sheltered location. The calm waters here make it an ideal spot for families with children. There are plenty of water sports facilities, including a windsurfing school, plus sunbeds and parasols to hire on the beach. Cala Millor's beach is considered one of the best in Majorca and is a haven for beach lovers and water sports enthusiasts.

A flag system is in operation in Cala Millor, and swimming is forbidden when a red flag is flying. There are boat trips available along the beach, including glass-bottomed boat trips…

Cala Millor

Cala Millor is a purpose-built resort and as such has been designed with holiday makers in mind, with a gorgeous promenade running along the beach, lined with palms and offering a wealth of shops, bars and restaurants catering to every taste.

There is a children's play area in the centre of town called Fantasy Park so there is plenty for the family to see and do in Cala Millor…

Cala Millor

In Cala Millor you are spoilt for choice when it comes to dining out, with lots of restaurants offering everything from traditional tapas and fresh seafood, to burgers, pub grub and all kinds of international menu's to pick from.

There are plenty of shops and boutiques in Cala Millor selling local crafts such as lace, leather goods and ceramics, as well as a good selection of shops selling beach accessories, and inflatable's. Nightlife is quite lively in Cala Millor, although not so hedonistic as the resorts of the south west, there are plenty of bars, discos and karaoke bars. There are plenty of options for family entertainment, with amusements and arcades along the promenade, as well as family friendly bars. If you fancy a change of scenery, it's possible to walk from Cala Millor to the quieter neighbouring resort of Cala Bona. Or, in the other direction, a longer stroll will take you to Sa Coma and S'Illot where Susie, Ginny and I stayed…

Cala Millor

If like us, you would like to see some of the islands wildlife then try a visit to the Punta Amer headland and nature reserve, with dramatic views and an old watchtower.

Set on a stunning long sandy beach, Cala Millor has everything required for a great family holiday in the sunshine so do not forget your bucket and spade…

Cala Ratjada

Discover a hidden holiday gem on Majorca's east coast that is Cala Ratjada which has the best of what Majorca has to offer for holiday makers.

Cala Ratjada is situated at the most eastern part of Majorca and is some 65 km (about 40 miles) from Palma International Airport…

Cala Ratjada

Cala Ratjada is set on a rugged peninsula surrounded by natural terrain and pine forests, in the municipal district of Capdepera, it is one of the more remote resorts in Majorca, and was originally a fishing village and port. Nowadays it is a well-established beach resort, with plenty of hotels, bars, restaurants, shops and amenities, and keeps one foot rooted in the past with its working harbour. The resort and surrounding area have several good sandy beaches with Blue Flag status to choose from. The main beach in Cala Ratjada is known as Son Moll. This is quite a small beach and can be quite busy in peak season, as can the other main beach in the resort, Cala Gat, also small.

The seawater is clear and calm, although it can shelve quite steeply in places, so those with children should be aware. You can also find excellent sandy beaches at nearby Cala Agulla and Cala Guya…

Cala Ratjada

Cala Ratjada is lined with shops bars and restaurants, many along the main promenade that runs along the beachfront of the resort. There are all kinds of cuisine on offer, from traditional Mallorcan fare to international cuisine and fast food.

The resort is quite lively and attracts young adults in groups so may not be suitable for young families or adults looking for a peaceful holiday location…

Cala Ratjada

Cala Ratjada village has an important role in Majorcan history, as it was the most used port on the east coast. This is the closest point to the neighbouring island of Menorca, and you can sometimes see Ciutadella, the major town on Menorca's west coast from here. You can also travel to Cuitadella from Cala Ratjada by hydrofoil. Other activities you can take part in while visiting the resort include golf, tennis, water sports and horse-riding.

The name Cala Ratjada means 'Bay of Rays', and the sun certainly shines around here. This is the bay for sun worshippers. The area is also protected as a special environmental area, and has a protected bird sanctuary…

Cala San Vicente

Cala San Vicente is a sleepy, traditional village on the north coast of Majorca, great for relaxing holidays enjoying sun, sand and seafood!

The picturesque village of Cala San Vicente is situated within the district of Pollensa, in the north of Majorca, about 60 km (approximately 37 miles) from Palma airport…

Cala San Vicente

Cala San Vicente is a traditional Mallorcan fishing village rather than a tourist resort. The pace of life here is sedate, and well suited to those seeking peace and quiet rather than a party holiday. This is a quiet destination, ideal for relaxing in the sun, and doing nothing much at all.

Set among rugged rocky coastline with magnificent views towards the Formentor peninsula, Cala San Vicente has three small beaches, connected by paths along the cliff tops. The largest beach, Cala Barques has sunbeds, parasols and pedaloes for hire. The other two beaches, Cala Molins and Cala Clara are also popular, and all can become quite crowded in peak season. Each sheltered cove has fine white sand gently shelving into clear sparkling seawater, and the area is well known as a good area to snorkel…

Cala San Vicente

Cala San Vicente has a small selection of bars, restaurants and shops catering to tourists, around the Cala Barques beach area. For dining out, there are a few excellent seafood restaurants selling the catch of the day, and a handful of bars around the village, all with a very friendly and welcoming atmosphere.

Spend time walking around the village itself and you'll see quaint houses and cobbled streets, a taste perhaps of times gone by…

Cala San Vicente

Attractions in Cala San Vicente are few and far between but this is a place to chill out and enjoy the peace and quiet. There is an interesting site worth a visit, a set of ancient man-made caves which date back to the Bronze Age, these are open to the public. The resort also has a mini-golf course, and there is a street market here each Sunday morning, selling fresh local produce and crafts. For a change of scenery, the pretty town of Pollensa where we stayed during one of our many holidays to the island is only 5 km away, with Puerto Pollensa and Alcudia are also within easy reach. Cala San Vicente is a pleasant and laid-back resort, best suited to couples or families with young children.

So for peace and quiet, try Cala San Vicente, set on a quiet stretch of Majorca's north coast. It is a traditional fishing village with a relaxed pace…

Calas De Mallorca

Calas De Mallorca is the place for a relaxing family holidays, it really fits the bill. It is small and friendly, with plenty of activities for children, it is a great spot for unwinding and re-charging your batteries.

Calas de Mallorca is a small, modern, purpose built resort situated on the rocky east coast of Majorca…

Calas De Mallorca

The resort itself enjoys a pleasant cliff-top setting, with three small sandy beaches set in sheltered coves, accessible via paths and steps that wind down the cliff side. It has spectacular views over the sea. Located in the district of Manacor and is approximately 70 km (about 44 miles) from Palma Airport. Calas de Mallorca is an ideal spot for a quiet, relaxing holiday, with low-key nightlife and a friendly, laid-back atmosphere.

It's a perfect place to hit the beach and chill out, and also a good base for those looking to explore the east of the island. In Calas de Mallorca there are three small beaches, each set in a rugged cove (cala), the largest being Cala Domingos Gran, which has European Blue flag status, sunbeds, parasols and water sports facilities such as pedaloes. The other two beaches, Cala Domingos Petit and Cala Antena also have the Blue Flag award, and also have similar facilities, and all three can become somewhat crowded in peak season…

Calas De Mallorca

Calas De Mallorca's beach is of soft and smooth sand, and the seawater is blue and crystal clear.

Adults with children and other people should be aware that there can be strong undercurrents in the sea in this area, so weak swimmers and children should stay closer to the beach at all times and not use inflatable's in the sea…

Calas De Mallorca

Most of the tourist facilities in Calas De Mallorca are set in one central area, the Centro Commercial (commercial centre), typical of the type found in many Majorca resorts. Here you will find a cluster of shops selling beachwear, souvenirs, crafts and holiday essentials, alongside cafes, bars, restaurants and amusements. You can also hire family fun bikes, scooters and cars from here. This is a great resort for families with children. It is nice and quiet and does not attract crowds of 18-30's and is therefore, not as noisy as some other resorts.

There is a children's playground and funfair in the commercial centre, with loads of activities including mini go-karts, bouncy castle, trampolines and climbing frames. There is also a fun little mini-golf course for all ages right in the middle of the commercial centre…

Calas De Mallorca

In Calas De Mallorca a tourist road train, the Calas Express, runs around the resort between the beaches, which is great fun for the kids and saves the legs of the adults.

Food and drink are easy to come by, with some excellent seafood restaurants as well as the usual array of international cuisine that you might expect in a purpose-built resort…

Calas De Mallorca

When you stay in Calas de Mallorca, you can explore the east coast very easily. There are some buses, although these are renowned for being a little unpredictable, so hiring a car may be the way to go in this part of Majorca. That said, taking the bus can be an adventure. You can travel by bus to Porto Cristo, or Manacor, home of Majorca's pearl industry. We went and had the tour of the factory and shop and enjoyed the experience.. It's also possible to get a bus from Calas de Mallorca to the Capital city of Palma. Also worth a visit if you're in this area is Felanitx market, acclaimed as the best in Majorca. Another place we have visited in the past and the market is well worth a visit.. This takes place each Sunday morning, and attracts visitors by the coach load to the vast array of stalls offering all kinds of souvenirs, pottery, clothing and good quality leather goods.

Family friendly, relaxing and with amazing views over the cliff tops, Calas de Mallorca is a chilled out resort on the east coast, with small, secluded beaches, ideal for family holidays…

Camp de Mar

This is the place to go for a truly relaxing beach holiday. Camp de Mar is in the south west of Majorca. The resort benefits from sun, sand and relaxation in gorgeous surroundings.

Camp de Mar is a small, quiet beach resort within the municipal district of Andratx, in the south west of Majorca. Situated approximately 32 km (about 20 miles) from Palma airport...

Camp de Mar

Camp de Mar is a picturesque and charming, the resort is located in a small bay and has a fine sandy beach gently sloping into the warm, clear seawater of the Mediterranean. Set amongst rocky headlands which seem to frame the view out over the sea, its location is one of the prettiest in Majorca and an ideal setting for a lazy beach holiday. Camp de Mar's tourist facilities include a handful of restaurants and bars, a sprinkling of souvenir and gift shops, and a few upmarket hotels.

Camp de Mar is far less developed than some of the other south west coast resorts, such as Palma Nova, Santa Ponsa or Magaluf. As such you will not find the same range of bars and restaurants; however there are some nice places to eat here, including seafood and traditional Majorcan cuisine. Evening entertainment in Camp de Mar is mainly hotel based. One attraction is the lovely floating 'island' beach bar, set on a rocky outcrop, and accessed via a jetty. What a place to enjoy a cocktail and take in the views…

Camp de Mar

The atmosphere in Camp de Mar is relaxed and peaceful, and is well-suited to families and couples seeking laid back holidays in a friendly location.

Although there are not many tourist attractions as such, the area is popular with countryside lovers as there is plenty to explore such as secluded coves, wooded hills and pine-clad valleys…

Camp de Mar

Camp de Mar has an exclusive feel, and attracts some rich and famous property owners. If you visit Camp de Mar you will notice a lot of very special looking villas, many owned by celebrities. There are quite a few villas in the area, and the resort tends to attract independent travellers owning or renting privately, rather than package holiday makers.

All in all, Camp de Mar is a quiet, exclusive resort where you can kick back and relax. It has lovely scenery, great beach, and beautiful countryside. Not a resort if you want a lively atmosphere. For a change of scenery, try neighbouring Paguera just to the east, or Andratx and Puerto Andratx to the north and west. So for relaxation, peace and quiet, try Camp de Mar, a small beach resort in the south west of the island…

Can Pastilla

Can Pastilla is a relaxed family resort set on the south coast, with a picturesque marina, golden sandy beach and a welcoming atmosphere.

Can Pastilla is the closest resort to the city of Palma and is just 2 km away from Palma airport…

Can Pastilla

Can Pastilla is fairly quiet (apart from some aircraft noise) resort and shares a glorious stretch of beach along the south coast with neighbouring resorts Playa de Palma and El Arenal, both of which are within walking distance. The beach here slopes gently into the sea, which is clear and warm, and has amenities such as toilets, showers and snack bars dotted at regular intervals along the entire stretch of beach. You will also find plenty of sunbeds and parasols for hire, as well as water sports.

Like many of Majorca's resorts, Can Pastilla has evolved from a small fishing village into a well-established holiday resort with all the amenities. There is still a flavour of authentic Mallorca with winding, narrow streets and the pretty parish church of the Church of Sant Antonio de la Playa…

Can Pastilla

Can Pastilla has a pretty marina and is usually full of bobbing boats and yachts and a lovely place to wander around in the early evening.

Can Pastilla is well served by a good array of bars, restaurants and cafes serving everything from local Mallorcan cuisine and seafood to international options and pub grub…

Can Pastilla

This relaxed resort is very suitable for family holidays, and is popular with British tourists and ex-pats. It's a reasonable quiet resort, less boisterous than neighbouring El Arenal which tends to attract young holiday makers. If you fancy a change, you can walk or cycle to neighbouring resorts quite easily, or alternatively why not jump on the tourist mini-train which runs from Can Pastilla to El Arenal, passing through Playa de Palma.

This is an ideal place to stay on holiday if you want to experience the delights of Majorca's capital city, with Palma just a short drive away. One thing to note about Can Pastilla is of course, being so close to the airport, there is some noise from aircraft particularly in the western side of the resort. For relaxing family beach holidays, you needn't look further than Can Pastilla, just 2 km from Palma airport, with a sandy beach, a marina and a short walk to neighbouring Playa de Palma…

Ca'n Picafort

Ca'n Picafort is a laid-back sun-lovers resort on the east coast of Majorca. Set at the eastern end of the Bay of Alcudia, it has a fantastic, clean beach with safe, clear seawater, making it an excellent choice for families and sun-seeking holiday makers of all ages. Making this is a great bucket and spade resort.

Ca'n Picafort is located in the north east and about 62 km from Palma Airport…

Ca'n Picafort

Can Picafort is a resort with a very chilled out atmosphere, perfect for a relaxing beach holiday. The resort has a fabulous 3 km stretch of beach, a small fishing harbour and marina, and a long, spacious beach side promenade lined with cocktail bars and restaurants. In common with many of Majorca's resorts, the resort has grown from a small fishing village into a well-established tourist resort with all the amenities you would expect for a great holiday.

Can Picafort's location within the vast, stunning Alcudia Bay means that it benefits from the same wonderful soft sandy beach that you find in Puerto Alcudia, and has splendid views of the rocky Cabo del Pinar headland. The sands of Can Picafort beach shelve gently into the crystal clear sea, and there is plenty of space on the beach. There are ample sun loungers and parasols for hire along the beach, plus water sports and other facilities…

Ca'n Picafort

Ca'n Picafort is in the region of Santa Margalida which has over 150 officially recognised archaeological sites and many of which are pre-Roman so there is plenty here for those interested in history.

If you are not into history then there are plenty of shops of all kinds along the seafront promenade, and in the surrounding streets of Ca'n Picafort, so there's always something or other to capture your interest as you stroll along in the sunshine. There are also street markets on Tuesdays and Fridays…

Ca'n Picafort

There are plenty of bars and restaurants in Ca'n Picafort serving up all kinds of international fare, from traditional Spanish dishes to full English breakfasts and fast food, you can find whatever you fancy. There are also plenty of bars to choose from in Ca'n Picafort, including some fabulous cocktail bars along the seafront promenade, where you can sip a pina colada (or whatever you fancy) and take in the gorgeous views out over the sea to the Cabo del Pinar headland.

It is truly a relaxing place to holiday and you know you're on holiday when you're in Ca'n Picafort, it's so chilled out! There are a couple of nightclubs in the town for those wishing to live it up all night, but on the whole the nightlife is laid back…

Ca'n Picafort

Everyday of your holiday will not have to be spent on the beach and if you fancy a change of scenery, you can take a bus from Can Picafort to Puerto Alcudia along the coast road, via Playa de Muro.

For those who just want lazy chilled-out days sipping cocktails in the sun, Ca'n Picafort is the holiday destination for you. Its beach side promenade, the soft sandy beach and the relaxed, friendly atmosphere will ensure a holiday to remember. Ca'n Picafort is a great destination for family beach holidays as it is clean, has white sand and has safe, clear seawater, with everything you may need close by…

Colonia Sant Jordi

For a quiet, relaxed beach holiday, Colonia Sant Jordi really hits the mark as it is un-spoilt and has a easy-going atmosphere, in an area with fantastic beaches.

Colonia Sant Jordi is situated on the south east coast of Majorca, in a fairly remote spot, some 40 km from Palma and the airport…

Colonia Sant Jordi

The un-spoilt town is set on a gorgeous stretch of coast line, Colonia Sant Jordi tends to attract independent travellers, and is mostly ignored by major tour operators. This means it is something of a hidden gem, although not a traditional Mallorcan fishing village like so many other resorts around the island. As its name suggests, this resort was originally a colony set up in the 19th century for agriculture and fishing, which then developed and adapted to tourism.

There is a small but very pretty beach, Sa Platja des Port, which has tourist facilities such as sunbeds and parasols. There are also several excellent alternative beaches in the area, including a nudist beach at Es Trenc. along with Es Dolc and Sa Rapita, which is a stunning beach, indeed all three are renowned for their natural beauty. So there is plenty to see and enjoy around this resort....

Colonia Sant Jordi

Colonia Sant Jordi has beaches that are flanked with pine forests, these are very picturesque, and are said to resemble beaches in the Caribbean, with amazing white sand and turquoise sea.

The resort is quiet and un-commercialised, with a handful of nice restaurants and bars, mainly around the marina area, so it is a destination for sun-lovers looking for a relaxing holiday rather than party-goers. There are a few tourist shops from which you can buy beachwear, souvenirs and a street market each Wednesday. So this is a great place to take your bucket and spade and make sand castles with the children…

Colonia Sant Jordi

Colonia Sant Jordi also has a small fishing harbour and a marina, from which you can take a boat to Cabrera Island, a National Park nature reserve which is a small, rocky island of just 6 square miles. Due to its protected status, building is forbidden, and so Cabrera has no facilities, it's simply a place to explore and take in the nature and history of the place. There is a good range of holiday accommodation options in Colonia Sant Jordi, with a selection of hotels and apartments in the resort.

Alan in the sea…

You can also find private apartments and villas here, for a little more luxury or privacy. Colonia Sant Jordi is within the municipality of Ses Salines, which takes its name from the area's long history of salt extraction, said to go back to Roman times. For those wanting to explore more of Majorca, you can catch a bus from Colonia Sant Jordi to Palma, although the timetables here can be a bit unreliable. This is a good base for anyone wishing to explore the south of Majorca. Visit Colonia Sant Jordi for lazy, relaxed beach holidays away from the crowds…

Deia

If you are looking for something out of the ordinary: Deia is a place where time stands still, picturesque, cultured and magical.

Deia is a very pretty cliff side village on the west coast of Majorca, about 35 km (about 20 miles) from Palma airport…

Deia

Situated in the midst of the Sierra Tramuntana mountain range, Deia is a maze of steep, winding, narrow streets and paths, with fantastic views out over the rugged coastline to the sea. The skyline above is dominated by mountains. Teix being the highest, which is over 1000 metres above sea level is the second highest on Majorca. Deia is a charming and pretty place, with plenty to see and do. The village has an attractive 15th century church, which houses a collection of religious art. Narrow cobbled streets offer plenty to see and do, with art galleries, workshops and stylish boutiques. There are a few bars and restaurants, with amazing atmosphere, offering authentic Mallorcan cuisine and tapas, and local liqueurs like hierbas.

The village itself is small and has an exclusive feeling and it attracts many day trippers, yet remains free of hordes of holiday makers making this a great place to stay…

Deia

In Deia the holiday accommodation here is mainly private villas and holiday homes.

There is a luxury hotel, La Residencia in Deia, made up of two restored stately houses and if you can afford to stay here, it is a lovely place to enjoy all that the village has to offer…

Deia

Many who do stay here for a holiday use it as a base for exploring the mountains and down the whole of the western coast. Set deep in lush green countryside, packed with pine forests, citrus and olive groves, the surrounding area has a wealth of countryside footpaths. This area attracts walkers, cyclists and nature lovers, with challenging routes and fabulous scenery. There is a small, pebbled beach in Deia, and it is possible to walk along a challenging coastal path to Puerto de Soller. From there you can take a tram up the hillside to Soller town and even a train to Palma if you so wish. We have used the train when we have holidayed on Majorca in the past. It is called the "Orange Blossom Line" as it passes through orange groves on its way to Palma.

This is a place of dazzling beauty, and of art, culture and romance. Deia has long been a mecca for writers, musicians, artists and celebrities. So you never know who you may bump into!…

Deia

In Deia you can while away afternoons meandering around the winding, twisty streets set almost terrace-like on the hillside, with amazing views out over the sea. Deia has a significant place in Majorca's history as there has been a settlement on the site since at least the 10th century, and the coastal area close to the village was the site of a major battle in the 16th century. The islanders successfully defended against an invasion of Moors, and the battle is celebrated and re-enacted each year on the 13th May. Watchtowers built following the battle are still in place (ruins) to this day.

Visit Deia for a taste of something a little different as it is a quaint, pretty village on the west coast, with splendid views from the hillsides around…

El Arenal

El Arenal is a lively beach resort, with plenty of bars, clubs and discos and is perfect for partying all night long after a long lazy day on the beach. The resort may not suit families or those who are looking for a more peaceful location!

El Arenal is situated 10 km east of Palma de Mallorca, on Majorca's south coast and is a large well-established resort. Just 5 km from Palma International Airport…

El Arenal

This upbeat resort sits at the eastern end of a long stretch of sandy beach, along which sit the neighbouring resorts of Playa de Palma and Can Pastilla. The three resorts are linked by a long promenade along the coast, and almost blend into one, so you can easily walk between them. The walk is a pleasant one without any hills, so is fine for pushchair's, wheelchairs etc., and also an easy route for cycling along. You can hire bicycles from several places in the resorts. There is also a tourist mini-train that runs between the three resorts during the summer season.

El Arenal has plenty of facilities along its stretch of this fabulous sandy beach, which has Blue Flag status. There are plenty of water sports and pedalo hire, sunbeds and parasols, plus beach huts (Balnearios) dotted along at regular intervals providing drinks and snacks, showers and toilet facilities. There's also a wealth of cocktail bars, restaurants and cafes along the beachfront promenade…

El Arenal

Other activities in El Arenal include tennis courts, mini golf (Golf Fantasia), boat trips, scuba diving, sailing and a water park and Aqua land.

El Arenal has a wealth of lively bars and clubs and has a very lively atmosphere and nightlife…

El Arenal

El Arenal is a loud resort and not the place to come if you are seeking relaxation and peace and quiet. Holiday accommodation in the resort spans the full range from budget accommodation to luxury hotels, self-catering to all-inclusive. Many are adult-only, reflecting the hard-partying nature of El Arenal. There is plenty of choice for eating out, with a full range of international restaurants, including traditional Spanish, German and British.

For exploring beyond the resort, transport links from Arenal to Palma are good and there are regular buses, and it's a relatively short journey, so taking a taxi is also a viable option if you wish to do some city sightseeing or shopping. For loud and lively nightlife, El Arenal has it all, a resort for party lovers, with a fantastic sandy beach and plenty of activities…

Illetas

Illetas is a hidden gem on the island of Majorca's south west coast. Exclusive, affluent and picturesque, an upmarket beach resort that's ideal for luxury beach holidays.

Situated on a cliff side close to Palma Bay, Illetas is within the municipal district of Calvia, and at just 10 km (about 6 miles) from Palma Airport…

Illetas

The resort of Illetas is considered to be one of the most exclusive on the island and this is certainly reflected in the class of hotels, restaurants and bars in the resort. Most of the hotels in Illetas are luxury hotels aimed at affluent tourists, and there is a sophisticated feel to the resort with classy cafes, bars and restaurants.

There is a small sandy beach at Illetas, as well as several rocky coves. The beach does get busy but you can usually find a quiet spot for yourself on the soft white sand. The sea is warm and clear and very inviting. Illetas is not typically a destination for package holiday makers and few tour operators offer package holidays here. In the main, holiday makers in this town tend to be independent travellers, families and couples looking for something a little more refined than some of Majorca's more well-known resorts. There are few tourist attractions and the resort will appeal more to those seeking peace and quiet. The atmosphere is relaxed and laid back so this is not the place for activities, noisy entertainment or all night parties…

Illetas

Illetas has regular buses that go to Palma and around the south west, so Illetas is a good base for exploring. Its proximity to the city of Palma also means that a lively night out is within easy reach, just a short taxi ride away. The resort of Cala Mayor is also close by. The rugged cliffs and greenery set around mainly low-rise buildings, Illetas is a pretty resort with stunning views of the surrounding area and Mediterranean sea. Its exclusive feel and luxury facilities will appeal to the more discerning holiday maker.

Exclusive and upmarket, the beach resort of Illetas is a hidden gem on Majorca's south west coast, within half an hour of the airport…

Magaluf

We have holidayed in Magaluf in the past and enjoyed the exciting feel of the nightlife and found that the beach was lovely to relax on by day. When the children grew up we wanted a more peaceful holiday so went to other more relaxing resort on the island. As we do agree that Magaluf is a lively party resort, and it doesn't disappoint. Fun, sun and clubbing are the order of the day here.

The very popular and well-established holiday resort of Magaluf, along with its close neighbours, Palma Nova and Torrenova, occupies a peninsula on the south west coast of Majorca, within the district of Calvia. Magaluf is about 15 km from Palma airport and benefits from great beaches and night life…

Magaluf

The resort has been improved in recent years to upgrade the beach and beachfront area. Several high rise buildings have been demolished and the addition of a palm lined promenade has helped improve the look and feel of the resort. This is a lively resort by anyone's standards, and has a reputation for wild nightlife, typically the British 18-30 crowd and young groups of revelers. Magaluf attracts a large number of hen and stag parties, and has a somewhat saucy reputation and is often referred to as Shagaluf! There are several big nightclubs and discos in Magaluf, open all night, so there is never a dull moment. The most famous club is probably BCM, which attracts famous DJs.

Karaoke and discos are very popular in Magaluf and it can be very loud place so it is not for the faint hearted...

Magaluf

The atmosphere in Magaluf is generally friendly and the resort is proud of its fun, party town reputation, whilst still welcoming and friendly enough to attract families. The beach at Magaluf is beautiful, white and sandy and has plenty of amenities. You can hire sunbeds and parasols, banana boats, pedaloes and more. There are all kinds of boat trips and water sports available, including jet-skiing and windsurfing, plus scuba diving. The water is clean warm and clear, and the shores slope gently, making a very safe beach for children. Lifeguards are in attendance.

The resort itself has plenty of everything. It is buzzing with bars, cafes, restaurants, fast food outlets, nightclubs and discos. There are a great number of British pubs here too, many serving pub grub and full English breakfasts…

Magaluf

There are plenty of shops in Magaluf that are selling clothing, beach accessories, souvenirs, jewellery, and leather goods and virtually everything you could need on holiday.

Holiday accommodation options in Magaluf range from budget self-catering or room-only apartments to luxury and all-inclusive hotels…

Magaluf

The resort of Magaluf has lots of no-frills accommodation options, and there are plenty of cheap holiday deals to Magaluf, no doubt this helps its continuing popularity with young adult holiday makers on a budget.

There are also plenty of family friendly hotels in the resort with in-house entertainment and children's clubs…

Magaluf

Although like us, many families do visit Magaluf, Palma Nova may be a better option for those with young children, away from the liveliest of the nightlife. Out of season, Magaluf sees less of the hen and stag parties, and more families and couples seeking winter breaks, although many party groups do still visit Magaluf for the weekend. There is a water park in Magaluf, Aqua land, and you'll also find mini-golf ,tennis and horse-riding amongst the things to do in the resort. There is also a world renowned Pirates Show featuring pyrotechnics and acrobatics to see.

Palma Cathedral.

From Magaluf, it's easy to explore a little further afield, with good public transport links in the area, including regular buses to Palma City. You can easily walk into Palma Nova and Torrenova as they practically merge into one resort. For all-night clubbing and bouncing nightlife, Magaluf is the place with a lively beach resort, packed with bars and clubs, with plenty of family amenities too, and a friendly, fun atmosphere…

Paguera

Paguera is a friendly and very clean resort and has plenty to offer the holiday maker of all ages, with three sandy beaches and lively nightlife.

Paguera is a modern tourist resort in the south west of Majorca, in the district of Calvia. Some 35 km (about 20 miles) from Palma Airport…

Paguera

Like many of Majorca's popular holiday resorts, Paguera has developed from a small fishing village into a tourist-orientated town, and is particularly popular with German tourists.

The resort is a clean and well laid-out with three beaches, Playa Palmira, Playa Tora, and Playa La Romana, each of which has plenty of facilities for sunbathing and water sports. This is a good choice for a family holiday…

Paguera

Paguera has blue flag status beaches which are joined by a pedestrian promenade which runs along the seafront. Paguera is noted for its cleanliness and the resort is maintained very well and is a very pleasant place to wander around. The beaches are all clean and sandy, with gently shelving sands sloping into clear warm seawater, and plenty of space for families to enjoy their own spot of beach. There are plenty of shops, bars, restaurants and cafes along the main street that runs the full length of the resort. This is a great bucket and spade resort.

Paguera is a fairly lively resort, it has plenty of nightlife and is not especially recommended if you are seeking peace and quiet, as there are several discos that stay open until the early hours. As well as being popular with German tourists, the resort also attracts many British holiday makers, and there are a number of British bars and cafes in the resort, catering to British tastes, for example serving full English breakfasts and the usual pub grub…

Paguera

Paguera has plenty of fine dining options with some international dining menus and of course some traditional Spanish cuisine including fresh fish and other seafood.

Around Paguera there are a number of notable hiking routes through the surrounding countryside, so it is a good base for anyone who enjoys exploring a little bit further afield…

Paguera

Paguera itself is conveniently located for visits to Andratx market, and the stylish coastal resort of Port d'Andratx. You can also take boat trips around the coast or to the island of Dragonera, which is a nature reserve with Roman ruins and a small museum. One thing to note if you are considering a holiday in Paguera is that the resort is quite hilly, and many of the hotels and apartments are uphill so may be challenging for anyone with a pushchair, wheelchair or mobility issues.

Paguera is a well-established holiday resort in south west Majorca, with three gorgeous beaches and plenty of nightlife and activities...

Palma Nova

Palma Nova is where a fun-packed family holiday is guaranteed, with gorgeous sandy beach, activities galore and short transfer time from the airport, Palma Nova has it all. The sea is always very welcoming and there is plenty of room on the beach for everyone.

Palma Nova is a large, well-established and popular resort in Calvia, in the south west of Majorca, just about 15 km from Palma airport…

Palma Nova

Palma Nova is a modern purpose-built resort with little in the way of a traditional Majorca feel but it has every amenity a holiday maker might need. Palma Nova, along with its close neighbours, Torrenova and Magaluf, is extremely popular with British tourists, indeed the three resorts almost merge into one and it is easy to walk between them almost by accident. When we holidayed in Magaluf we often wandered down to Palma Nova beach to spend the day swimming and sand castle building with the children.

Palma Nova attracts many families year after year, no doubt due to its impressive beach and facilities. The upbeat, friendly vibe and huge selection of bars and restaurants makes Palma Nova a mecca for sun lovers and party-goers alike. There is plenty going on here yet the pace is a little gentler than neighbouring Magaluf. There is one all-night disco, although Magaluf is a short walk away, and the place to go for clubbing holidays. That said, nightlife in Palma Nova is upbeat and lively, with a great choice from music bars and discos to family entertainment such as cabaret, karaoke and bingo. There are plenty of English, Irish and Scottish bars here, reflecting the popularity of the resort with British holiday makers…

Palma Nova

There are three beaches in Palma Nova called the main, central beach and the Playa de Palma Nova, which tends to be the busiest.

In Palma Nova there are plenty of facilities such as sun loungers and parasols for hire, and all kinds of water sports facilities so there is plenty here for all ages and tastes…

Palma Nova

In Palma Nova all of the beaches have Blue Flag status, and are very clean, tidy, and well-equipped, with fine white sand. The shoreline slopes very gently into the sea which is clear and clean. There is also a small marina. Palma Nova is a superb destination for water sports fans. Active holidays start here, with all kinds on offer from windsurfing to banana boats, pedaloes to jet-skiing. There are also countless boat trips available, including glass bottomed boats. For eating out, you're spoiled for choice in Palma Nova, with every imaginable international cuisine on offer, from traditional Mallorcan to fast food, and everything in-between!

The resort of Palma Nova enjoys a pretty promenade along the seafront, lined with shops, bars and restaurants. You can buy all kinds of swim wear, beach accessories, souvenirs, crafts, leather goods and gifts. There is no street market here, but you can take a bus, like us, to Andratx market, which is held each Wednesday morning to enjoy the shopping experience of an open air market…

Palma Nova

When holidaying in Palma Nova if you fancy a change of scenery, it's easy and quick to travel by bus to the city of Palma, where cultural sights, fantastic shopping and trendy bars await you! You must really try to drag yourself away from the beach and visit the capital of the island as it is well worth the effort.

Palma Nova has all the ingredients for a lively family holiday by the beach, with bucket loads of entertainment options and much, much more…

Playa De Muro

Playa De Muro is a small, rather secluded resort on the north east coast of Majorca, within the vast Bay of Alcudia with miles of soft white sand edging the coastline. It is a delightfully peaceful and exclusive getaway destination.

Playa De Muro is a quiet, modern resort some 60 km from Palma Airport, Playa De Muro shares the same stretch of coastline as the resorts of Alcudia and Can Picafort…

Playa De Muro

Playa De Muro resort spans a stretch of fabulous white sandy beach with plenty of space for sunbathing and playing with the children. It has soft clean sand sloping gently into clear warm blue seawater and the beach is great for families with young children. Water sports facilities are available, such as windsurfing and jet-ski hire, as are sun loungers and parasols. There are also boat trips available from Playa De Muro. A quiet, fairly relaxed resort, Play de Muro has a more exclusive feel than its neighbours Alcudia and Can Picafort. Most of the hotels here are four or five star and the resort tends to cater for the more upmarket holiday maker, with all-inclusive deals being very popular. Stroll along the promenade and you will enjoy fabulous views of the bay and the sparkling Mediterranean Sea.

The resort has a small selection of shops selling beachwear, accessories and souvenirs, and also has a street market on Saturdays which is well worth a visit…

Playa De Muro

The resort of Playa De Muro also has a selection of bars, restaurants and cafes, including some British and other internationally-themed restaurants as well as more traditional Spanish dining options.

Playa de Muro is a relatively undiscovered and exclusive spot, ideal for anyone seeking a peaceful, relaxing holiday, and is family friendly with activities such as a maze in the resort centre. Nearby S'Albufera Park is a wildlife and nature reserve on the outskirts of Playa de Muro which is visited by serious bird-lovers as well as attracting families for a day out. Chill out and kick back in secluded Playa de Muro, set within the huge Bay of Alcudia, with sandy white beach and a great family atmosphere and you will have a holiday to remember…

Playa De Palma

Playa De Palma is a beach holiday with everything you need on the doorstep, it is a well-equipped resort with a fabulous sandy beach and is just a short trip from the airport.

Playa de Palma sits in the centre of a long sandy stretch of coastline on the south of Majorca, along with the neighbouring resorts of Can Pastilla and El Arenal. About 10 km from the capital city of Palma, this beach resort is easy to get to from the airport and is very popular with visitors from many different countries…

Playa De Palma

Playa De Palma has a stunning stretch of beach with white sand. The beach has Blue Flag status, and is clean and safe, with a gentle incline into the warm clear seawater. There are plenty of facilities, including sun loungers and parasols for hire, water sports and snack kiosks, known as balnearios, which are dotted along the whole bay. Here you can buy drinks and snacks, and use shower and toilet facilities. From Playa de Palma there are good transport links to the neighbouring resorts of El Arenal in the east, and Can Pastilla to the west.

Alan in the sea…

The three resorts are joined by a wide, flat promenade, and the resorts are quite close together so they seem to almost merge into one resort, so it is no problem walking between them. There is also a tourist mini road train that travels between the three resorts providing an easier way to get around. Situated between El Arenal and Can Pastilla, Playa de Palma enjoys a good mixture of international holiday makers and is less focused towards any particular nationality (the other two resorts being favoured by German and British tourists respectively)…

Playa De Palma

There are plenty of bars, cafes and restaurants in Playa De Palma serving up a range of international cuisine, and a few that serve more traditional Spanish and Mallorcan dishes.

There are also many shops selling beachwear and accessories, holiday essentials and souvenirs in Playa De Palma so there are plenty of shopping opportunities available in this resort…

Playa De Palma

Playa de Palma is a great base for a beach holiday, with lots of accommodation options, from budget to luxury. There is a wealth of supermarkets and good value dining options to complement the many self-catering facilities, which sit alongside four and five star all-inclusive hotels. Most facilities in the resort, including hotels, are situated pretty close to the palm lined beachfront and the area is quite flat making this a very accessible resort for anyone with wheelchairs or push chairs.

From Playa de Palma it is only a short trip back into the city of Palma, Majorca's capital city which has plenty of shopping and sightseeing opportunities. There are regular buses to Palma city throughout the day. For beach holidays, look no further than Playa de Palma with sandy white beach, plenty of bars, cafes and restaurants and a lovely promenade…

Puerto Pollensa

We had a great holiday when we stayed in Puerto Pollensa some years ago and we loved it. We would often walk into the town which is a stunningly beautiful town packed with cultural and historical delights.

The old town of Pollensa is situated in northern Majorca, and like many of Majorca's towns, was built inland from its port area. Four miles to the east, the port area of Puerto Pollensa has itself developed into a major beach resort and attracts many holiday makers every year…

Puerto Pollensa

Pollensa town itself sits within an area of spectacularly beautiful countryside, close to the northern part of the Serra de Tramuntera mountain range. Packed with pretty, winding streets and traditional Mallorcan style low-rise buildings, this is arguably the most beautiful town in Majorca. All around are spectacular contrasting views of lush green rural landscapes, pine forests, mountains, craggy cliffs and then the gorgeous deep blue waters of the Mediterranean Sea.

This is a great area for exploring, rambling and cycling, whether you prefer a leisurely afternoon stroll or something more challenging. As well as the stunning scenery, Pollensa has plenty to offer visitors seeking culture, history and medieval architecture. The vibe is quite cosmopolitan and chic. Pollensa is a more traditional town than many of the modern resorts on the island, providing a marked contrast to some of the other larger resorts. This is an arty and stylish town, with art galleries, chic boutique shops and cafes and plenty of character…

Puerto Pollensa

Pollensa, like many Mallorcan towns, has a central plaza which is the focal point of the town and is at the foot of an ancient stone staircase known as the Calvari steps, of which there are 365 steps so there is one for everyday of most years.

You will find that in the centre of the plaza in Pollensa is a fountain, and the square is lined with cafes and restaurants…

Puerto Pollensa

Pollensa is blessed with a great number of fine restaurants, with a wide variety of local and international cuisine and fine wines. Fresh local produce is in abundance everywhere. The town is also home to a beautiful church, Nostra Senyora Del Angels (Our Lady of the Angels). Another notable church in Pollensa is the Gothic church of Sant Jordi, and in Pollensa there are several ancient chapels. A weekly street market is held in Pollensa town on Sunday mornings, when the square is packed with stalls offering local produce and crafts. You will find a good selection of fresh fruit, vegetables, meat, fish, seafood, plus locally grown olives and olive oil.

The town also comes alive for celebrations and festivals throughout the year. For some beach time, head down to Puerto Pollensa, where you will find plenty to see and do. Pollensa is a pretty, old town, packed with cultural delights, from historic relics to art galleries and nature trails…

Portals Nous

Peaceful and secluded, Portals Nous is a quiet laid-back resort, with a charming marina and host of classy cafes and restaurants, ideal for chilled out holidays away from the crowds.

Portals Nous is a small, remote resort in the district of Calvia, in south west Majorca. Conveniently located, just 15 km from Palma Airport…

Portals Nous

The resort of Portals Nous has a very relaxed vibe and is a world away from neighbouring resorts such as Magaluf. This is a place to come and relax in. There are plenty of cafes, bars and restaurants in Portals Nous serving a good selection of international and Mallorcan cuisine, in particular the fresh fish and seafood dishes that Majorca is famous for. The area has several beaches, some with water sports, sunbeds and parasols. Other beaches have small secluded coves with few distractions. There is also a marina, Puerto Portals, which attracts beautiful yachts and is a great place to sit and take in the view. There are a number of nice restaurants and open air cafes around the waterfront when you need a rest or something to eat and drink.

There is a spectacular and renowned golf course in Portals Nous, the Royal Bendinat, complemented by breath-taking scenery. At just 10 km from the city of Palma, this is also a convenient base from which to explore the sights of the capital. However, public transport from Portals Nous is quite limited unlike the surrounding area which is generally quite well served. If you want to use this resort as a base for exploring the area around Calvia or Palma city, you should consider travelling by taxi or perhaps hiring a car…

Portals Nous

Portals Nous is also fairly close to several other major resorts, all of which could be explored by car, such as Santa Ponsa, Magaluf or Palma Nova, all close by in Calvia.

This is a peaceful resort with laid-back nightlife, ideal for a relaxing beach holiday. Portals Nous has just enough holiday ingredients to cater for your needs without ever being overbearing or overcrowded. The choice of beaches makes this a brilliant destination for family holidays, with or without children. For a relaxing beach holiday, Portal Nous has everything at hand, with a selection of bars, classy eateries and gorgeous sandy beaches…

Porto Colom

The first holiday we had on Majorca way back in the 1970's was spent at this resort and we like many others enjoyed the taste of having a peaceful, relaxing Majorcan holiday. Porto Colom is a small holiday resort with just enough facilities for a stress free break, away from the tourist hordes.

The village of Porto Colom is situated on the southern part of Majorca's east coast, within the district of Felanitx (there is a great market held in the town of Felanitx which we enjoyed visiting during our stay) and is around 70 km (about 44 miles) from the airport…

Porto Colom

Porto Colom is a small and relatively un-spoilt resort and is a traditional fishing village in common with many of Majorca's resorts, yet it has retained its original charm better than most, and has resisted aggressive development. As a result, Porto Colom is a pretty resort, offering a peaceful setting for relaxed family holidays, with a distinctly Spanish flavour. The village is set around a large harbour where you will still see a number of working fishing boats alongside the luxury yachts and speedboats. There are a few shops and bars around the marina area, so it's a good place to sit with a drink and watch the world go quietly by.

Alan in the sea…

There are several beaches in the area. At Porto Colom, Cala Marcal is a blue flag beach that is very pretty, with soft sands that shelve gently into the sea which is warm and clear, and very safe for children and toddlers. There are plenty of sun loungers and parasols for hire. Around Cala Marcal beach, you will see a handful of shops selling holiday essentials, beachwear and souvenirs, plus supermarkets for all your essentials. The hotel that we stayed in is located at Cala Marcal…

Porto Colom

There are also two smaller beaches near the harbour. The beach we used throughout our two weeks holiday to this resort is feature immediately below and was ideal for a bucket and spade family holiday.

If you have access to a car, there are also good beaches within a few miles…

Porto Colom

There are plenty of cafes, bars, and lovely restaurants in Porto Colom, including many around the harbour area, so you will have plenty of options for dining out. As with most of Majorca, you will find some amazing seafood restaurants serving the catch of the day. As far as tourist attractions go, the beach is the main draw here. Seclusion and quiet relaxation are the order of the day. So kick back, soak up the sun, eat, drink and chill out. Take a cliff side walk for amazing views of the bay, or a glass-bottomed boat trip. There is a street market held every Tuesday and Saturday morning, be sure to get there early to grab a bargain.

If history is your thing, you may be interested to know that Porto Colom is home to some of Majorca's oldest cultural sights. There is evidence of human life here dating as far back as 2000 BC, and there is also an important prehistoric burial site…

Porto Colom

Visit Porto Colom in mid-July and you can experience the festival known as La Verge del Carme called the feast of the patroness of fisher folk. This fiesta is celebrated with gusto and includes a celebratory dinner held on the beach. Holiday accommodation in Porto Colom ranges from self-catering apartments to four star hotels and private villas, so whatever your preference for accommodation, you will find something to suit your requirements.

Alan all at sea…

Porto Colom never gets over crowded, and is a lovely place to enjoy a peaceful, chilled out holiday as a couple or family, away from the hustle, bustle and noise of the major resorts. Visit Porto Colom for an enchanting getaway on Majorca's eastern coast, with sandy beach, harbour and the chance to visit some of the ancient sites of Mallorcan history…

Porto Cristo

Porto Cristo, a place were Susie, Ginny and I visited several times when we were staying nearby at Sa Coma, is a quiet relaxed and authentic village, with ancient sights and chic bars set around a working marina, an ideal spot for family fun on the beach.

Set on Majorca's east coast, Porto Cristo is a good 65 km (around 40 miles) away from Palma airport…

Porto Cristo

The town of Porto Cristo is a typical small Mallorcan fishing village, set around a natural harbour. Today you can still see working fishing boats in the harbour, alongside speedboats and yachts. Porto Cristo is quiet and does not have many activities, so is best for relaxed holidays, and is great for families. The resort is quite hilly, with a lot of steps, and may not be suitable for anyone with mobility problems, or wheelchair/ pushchair users.

There is a lovely beach, Cala Mandia, and several smaller coves dotted around the area. Nightlife is pretty quiet and laid back, with a few bars and restaurants offering a reasonable range of cuisine, mainly focused around the harbour area. Travel north a little to Cala Millor for a livelier scene with more bars and discos. There are a handful of hotels and apartment complexes, however this resort has not been over-developed and things are pretty low-key. Shops and supermarkets provide all the essentials you may need for self-catering holidays, and there are plenty of places to buy local crafts and souvenirs as well as clothing, beachwear and accessories…

Porto Cristo

Porto Cristo has an important place in Majorca's rich heritage and has numerous legends associated with it, included many suggestions on how the town earned its name (The Port of Christ). This was an important settlement for Christians in the 13th century.

The area is the site of many archaeological finds, including a prehistoric burial site, a Roman basilica and remnants of a Roman port. From Porto Cristo, it is not too far to visit the Caves of Drach and also the Manacor Pearl factory and Susie, Ginny and I did just that when we were staying at Sa Coma a few years ago. The resorts of Cala Millor and Calas de Mallorca are within driving distance to the north and south respectively. For peaceful, laid back getaways, Porto Cristo has everything you need. Lovely beach, working marina, and plenty of bars and restaurants, yet it remains small, un-spoilt and charming…

Puerto de Soller

One day during a recent holiday we went to Palma and caught the train from Palma to Soller and then we went on to visit Puerto de Soller which is a charming and picturesque coastal resort. Ideal for family holidays, the resort has a traditional feel, a distinctive tram, and a friendly welcoming atmosphere that's sure to win you over.

The coastal village of Puerto de Soller and its marina are situated in a picturesque horseshoe-shaped bay, enclosed by rocky headlands typical of Majorca's rugged west coast…

Puerto de Soller

Puerto de Soller was originally the port area built to defend the nearby town of Soller, and has evolved to cater for tourists. It is now considered a resort in its own right, although it is not over-developed and has a very definite charm of its own. It has a traditional feel, and is friendly, safe and welcoming.

Popular with walkers and independent holiday makers, the area attracts walkers, climbers and nature lovers, and there are plenty of walking trails around the Soller area. Yet the resort also has plenty to offer visitors seeking nothing more than sun, sea and sand…

Puerto de Soller

Puerto de Soller has two sandy beaches. Es Traves is the larger beach, at about 800 m in length. Ca'n Repic is a much smaller, narrower beach, and the two are joined by a wide pedestrian promenade so you can easily walk between the two and enjoy the views out to sea.

Both of the beaches have plenty of soft white sand, perfect for sunbathing on. Plenty of sunbeds and parasols are available for hire and the beaches do not get overcrowded so there is plenty of room for your sand castles…

Puerto de Soller

In Puerto de Soller there are plenty of cafes, bars and restaurants along the pretty promenade, and of course supermarkets and shops selling gift ware and souvenirs, beach essentials, clothing and footwear. Puerto de Soller has a lovely atmosphere, very relaxing and peaceful, with amazing views. You will find a selection of activities in the resort. From boat trips and diving excursions to windsurfing, banana boats, jet-skiing, and pedaloes so there really is something for everyone.

The Soller region is very beautiful, with fabulous landscapes and views all around. The area is set right at the heart of the Sierra de Tramuntana mountain range, and Majorca's highest mountain, Puig Mayor, is a dominant feature on the landscape in the Soller area. There is a lighthouse at the harbour entrance, known as El Faro. Puerto de Soller has a tram service, the Orange Express, which operates between the resort's harbour and the town of Soller. The journey is very pleasant and scenic as the tram makes its way down to the coast, through fragrant orange groves. There is also, as already mentioned, a notable train service which operates between Soller and Palma, with distinctive mahogany carriages, another experience worth trying if only for the fantastic views and scenery along the way…

Puerto de Soller

Puerto de Soller is approximately 35 km (about 22 miles) from Palma Airport. Transfers to Soller and Puerto de Soller can be quite slow due to the winding, mountainous nature of the route.

For laid-back beach holidays or exploring Majorca's natural beauty, the Soller area has it all. Puerto de Soller has everything you could need for a relaxing break away from the hustle and bustle and a chance to unwind in a beautiful setting…

S'illot

Several years ago we had a holiday in S'illot and found it to be a place to relax and unwind in. It is seen by many to be one of Majorca's most chilled out beach resorts. Another year we holidayed in Sa Coma just a short stroll away and on both occassions enjoyed this part of Majorca very much.

S'illot is situated on the east coast of Majorca, within the municipal district of Sant Llorenç des Cardassar. The resort is approximately 65 km (about 40 miles) from Palma and the airport…

S'illot

S'illot is quieter than neighbouring Sa Coma, S'illot is a very pleasant beach resort, with just enough amenities for a relaxing holiday. The resort has a lovely promenade that runs right through it, lined with palm trees, and with a fair selection of bars, restaurants, cafes and shops.

The beach at S'Illot is very pretty, with soft sands and very calm, warm seawater that lap gently. There are plenty of facilities such as sunbeds and parasols for hire, and a choice of water sports. You'll find pedaloes and banana boats, plus windsurfing and other activities. When we stayed there we spent many a happy day on the beach and I practically enjoyed having paella at a local beach side restaurant for my evening meals on several occassions…

S'illot

You will find that the pace of life (including the nightlife) in S'illot is laid back and relaxed. There are few lively bars here, with evening entertainment mainly provided by the hotels. Once a small fishing village, S'Illot has evolved to cater for tourists, yet still retains that traditional Mallorcan feel, perhaps in part due to the well-controlled pace of development in the area. To this day, you can still see working fishing boats in and around the fishing port area near the beach at S'Illot. There are several green zones around the village, some of which are classed as areas of special environmental interest, notably, the Punta de n'Amer headland.

Palma Shopping…

For a change of scenery, consider visiting the neighbouring resorts of Cala Millor or Sa Coma, or perhaps a trip further afield to Palma, all served by buses from S'Illot, although the bus timetables on this part of the island can be somewhat unreliable! Chill out and unwind in S'Illot in the small, relaxed beach resort on the east coast of Majorca…

Sa Coma

Sa Coma is the resort, on the island, where Susie, Ginny and I had our last Majorca holiday, staying in a hotel just set back from the beach. We spent a lot of time around the pool and on the beach during this holiday but did manage to go horse riding close by. We found that for a peaceful beach holiday with all the amenities and few crowds, Sa Coma was the perfect family holiday destination for us.

Sa Coma is a modern holiday resort, on Majorca's eastern coast, close to the larger resort of Cala Millor…

Sa Coma

Sa Coma is within the municipal district of Sant Llorenç des Cardassar, the resort is about 65 km (approximately 40 miles) from Palma airport. This is a fairly quiet resort that appeals to families. The beach is small but stunning, and no doubt a major draw for the many holiday makers who stay here each year.

Susie and Alan on holiday

Sa Coma has all the usual amenities: sun loungers and parasols, water sports equipment, pedaloes and other fun activities. The beach is clean and safe, a lovely place for children to play and splash. Along the seafront runs a pleasant promenade for pedestrians, along which you can walk almost the full length of the resort. The neighbouring resort of S'Illot is within walking distance and is a quieter, more traditional village, in contrast to Sa Coma. There is also a tourist mini-train that makes the journey between the resorts in the summer season. Sa Coma is a pleasant resort, purpose built yet not over-developed, and has a good array of facilities for holiday makers…

Sa Coma

We found that there are plenty of good bars, cafes and restaurants to choose from, and there was a family friendly atmosphere in the resort.

Sa Coma is a compact and friendly resort, it is not a traditional village and has little history or cultural attractions. It caters for holiday makers, pure and simple…

Sa Coma

Sa Coma attracts many British visitors and there are a good number of British bars and eateries. Nightlife is fairly restrained. There are some lively bars in the town, but on the whole things are not noisy after midnight. Much of the resort's entertainment is within the many hotel and apartment complexes. Nearby Cala Millor is within easy reach by taxi or a long stroll, and has more vibrant nightlife for those who like to party all night. Accommodation for holiday makers ranges from self-catering apartments and villas to good value 3 and 4 star hotels, some of which offer all-inclusive deals. Sa Coma also has a good selection of shops for souvenirs, beachwear and accessories. Local points of interest include the Punter De N'Amer headland, a specially protected area of great natural beauty.

Holidays in Sa Coma are quiet and relaxing, with a lovely beach and small selection of bars and restaurants, it is ideally suited to families…

Santa Ponsa

Santa Ponsa is a family resort on the South West coast of Majorca, in the municipal district of Calvia, close to Magaluf and Palma Nova. We have holidayed close by in Magaluf in the past and enjoyed the area very much.

The popular resort of Santa Ponsa is located about 26 km (approximately 16 miles) from Palma airport…

Santa Ponsa

Santa Ponsa is a very popular with European holiday makers, Santa Ponsa is a laid back and friendly resort, with beautiful sandy beaches, rocky coves and cliffs, a pine wood and a wealth of hotels, bars, cafes and restaurants. Santa Ponsa attracts visitors from England, Ireland, Scotland, Germany, Holland and Scandinavian. This gives the resort a cosmopolitan feel, and means that there is a great range of international cuisine available in Santa Ponsa's restaurants and cafes. From traditional Spanish cuisine and tapas, pizza, kebabs, ice cream, Scottish, Irish, English, Indian and Chinese, to MacDonalds and Burger King, there's every kind of food available in Santa Ponsa. The resort is especially popular with Irish and Scottish holiday makers, and this is reflected in the many Irish and Scottish bars, cafes and restaurants in the resort.

Nightlife in Santa Ponsa is mainly hotel-based but you will find family entertainment and live shows each evening in the "Spanish Square". The main strip on Calle Ramon de Montcada has an array of music bars, clubs, discos and restaurants, and after dark it becomes quite lively…

Santa Ponsa

Live music can be found at several venues around Santa Ponsa. This resort is perhaps not as full-on as the neighbouring Magaluf or Palma Nova but there is still plenty of fun to be had when the sun goes down in Santa Ponsa. If you are looking for an exciting and interesting place to base yourself than this resort could be for you …

Santa Ponsa

There are plenty of shops in Santa Ponsa, selling everything you could ever need on holiday such as beach accessories, clothing, shoes, handbags, leather goods, crafts, jewellery, T-shirts, sportswear, toys, gifts and souvenirs: there are shops running right along the road opposite the main beach, and also on the strip and in the commercial centre of the resort.

There are also several supermarkets in Santa Ponsa, with fresh fruit, bread and cakes and plenty of options for self-catering holiday makers. Many stock international brands so there is plenty of choice. Santa Ponsa is well-served by public transport, with regular (if not strictly to timetable!) buses to Palma via Magaluf and Palma Nova throughout the day. You can also get a bus to Marine Land from Santa Ponsa…

Santa Ponsa

Santa Ponsa's sandy main beach attracts plenty of sun seekers, both holiday makers and locals and it can be a little crowded, particularly a weekends but is ideal for young and old alike.

There are plenty of sunbeds and parasols for hire on the beach, and there are also several public toilets available along the beach. You will never be left without somewhere comfortable to sunbathe on Santa Ponsa beach…

Santa Ponsa

Santa Ponsa is a great base for those who like to explore the Mediterranean Sea, with diving, snorkelling and fishing all popular activities. The safe clear seawater, and gentle tides makes Santa Ponsa a swimmers and anglers delight.

Alan in the sea…

Santa Ponsa promenade runs along the main beach and is edged with pine trees and has a lovely pine wood at one end, where you can seek out the shade and watch the cute parakeets that live in the trees there. There is a rocky shoreline and lots of cliff paths around Santa Ponsa, and rocky coves perfect for rock pooling and splashing around in with the little ones. There is a roped-off restricted area for swimmers, where pedalo's, jet skis and boats are forbidden, it is recommended that swimmers stay within the restricted area to avoid risk of injury. Lifeguards are in attendance on the beach, and you must follow any instructions they give you. A flag system is in operation in Santa Ponsa, and swimming is forbidden when a red flag is flying. There is a first-aid post near the main beach, close to the tourist information centre…

Santa Ponsa

There is also a second, smaller beach in Santa Ponsa (known as the "little beach"), in a secluded cove, about 15 minutes walk from the main beach along Avenida Rey Jaime I. It has few facilities, but is a lovely spot for families, a sandy beach very gently sloping into shallow, calm, clear seawater.

An added bonus is that close to the little beach there is a nice children's play area to keep the little ones amused…

Santa Ponsa

A little further in the same direction and you will find Santa Ponsa Marina, Club Nautico Santa Ponsa. Close to the marina is a superb viewing spot, where you will see the Cruz de la Conquista monument. You can take boat trips from Santa Ponsa's main beach and marina. These take you around the south west coast and often include some time for diving and swimming, if you wish to do so. Points of architectural interest in Santa Ponsa include the Church of Nostra Senyora de l'Esperanca, and Chapel Sa Pedra Sagrada the Chapel of Sacred Stone. Sporting activities in Santa Ponsa include: tennis, bicycle hire, bungee, golf, diving, snorkelling, fishing, water-skiing, jet skiing and kite surfing. Around the resort you will find craft stalls, portrait and caricature artists, hair braiders, musicians and street entertainers. The resort really is a shoppers paradise.

The weather in Majorca makes it the perfect holiday destination for sun seekers and Santa Ponsa is no exception with year-round sunshine. The best of the sunny weather is from May to October, with cooler, less predictable weather from November to April…

Santa Ponsa

In Santa Ponsa in the peak summer months of July and August, it can be very hot and humid. Holiday makers to Majorca should take care to protect their skin from the strong sun. Always use sunscreen, even when it is cloudy or hazy, as the sun's rays are strong and you can still burn. I always wear sunglasses and a hat to add further protection so remember to stay safe and enjoy the sun in Santa Ponsa!

Santa Ponsa's sandy beaches and rocky coves make it a popular resort with European families. With plenty of sunshine, welcoming bars and restaurants and a great atmosphere, Santa Ponsa has something for everyone…

Santanyi

Santanyi is the ideal place for a laid back, upmarket holiday in a less-discovered part of Majorca, packed with cultural and historical delights.

The small, peaceful village of Santanyi is surrounded by beautiful countryside in the south east of the island…

Santanyi

The village of Santanyi is over 700 years old and has a perfect mixture of natural beauty and cultural attractions. This is a very peaceful holiday destination, and the village is not especially tourist-focused although visitors are made to feel very welcome in this relaxed and upmarket area of Majorca. Santanyi is a great place for soaking up the culture and local history.

This pretty village is packed with traditional architecture, rustic houses and cobbled streets, the skyline dominated by the Parish Church of Sant Andreu in the old quarter, which can be seen from miles around. Another notable feature is the Es Pontas stone arch at Cala Santanyi, the main beach set just outside of Santanyi. The coastline in this area is rocky and cragged, and tends to be dotted with coves. In Santanyi, the sea is crystal clear, vivid blue and very clean. There is an underwater cave here too, which is popular with divers. Elsewhere around the village you'll find gift shops and designer boutiques, so there are plenty of opportunities to buy souvenirs or crafts. There are a few art galleries around the village where you can view and also purchase artwork…

Santanyi

For eating out in Santanyi, there are a few options including a good selection of tapas bars and restaurants serving traditional Mallorcan cuisine as well as international dishes. Santanyi is a fairly secluded resort. Public transport is not really an option for exploring the area. If you hire a car during your holiday, you could take a short drive north to Cala d'Or for a change of scenery, or head south to visit the sleepy coastal village of Colonia Sant Jordi.

For a taste of the real Mallorcan culture and history, visit the village of Santanyi, in the south of the island…

Soller

We have already visited Puerto de Soller in this book but now it is time to go a little inland and visit the town of Soller. Here you can enjoy the true taste of traditional Majorca. Soller is a beautiful town in a dramatic setting, with mountains, fruit groves, and the fabulous horse-shoe bay of Puerto de Soller just a tram ride away.

Soller, in western Majorca, is set in a wide bowl-shaped valley surrounded by some of Majorca's most dramatic peaks. The town is about 3 km from the coast and the port area, Puerto de Soller…

Soller

Soller is a traditional old Mallorcan town, packed with history, architecture, and culture. Visit Soller and you will find plenty of old buildings: houses, public buildings and monuments, churches and museums to keep you occupied.

The focal point of the town, like so many in Majorca, is a central square, known as the Placa Constitucio, around which are situated a church, a town hall, and plenty of bars, restaurants, shops and boutiques so there is plenty to see and enjoy here for everyone…

Soller

Soller sits in an area that is known for its breath-taking scenery and natural beauty. Set in the western foothills of the Sierra de Tramuntana mountain range which covers much of the north and west of the island.

Soller is surrounded by lush green countryside, with lemon, orange and olive groves all around the area. Majorca's highest mountain, Puig Mayor, is a dominant feature on the landscape. Soller itself is a pretty town, packed with interesting buildings and streets. Some houses in the town date back as far as the 14th century. This is a great place for culture-seekers and those interested in Mallorcan history, as there are two museums here and plenty of monuments and historical buildings. Soller is a great base for exploring this whole area, and is popular with walkers and cyclists who use the many trails and pathways around the area to explore the countryside and take in some of the most stunning views on the island. The towns of Valldemossa, Deia and Alaro are all within easy reach by car. Soller's inland location means there are no beaches in the town itself, however it's just a short and scenic tram ride, the Orange Express, from Soller down to the coastal resort of Puerto de Soller, which has two sandy beaches…

Soller

The Orange Express distinctive orange tram carriages travel down the hillside to the beach area, so it's easy to access all of the delights that the port area has to offer, including a working harbour and a pretty promenade.

The best way to get between the two is undoubtedly this lovely tram journey, as the views are spectacular and the route takes you through fragrant orange groves…

Soller

Soller also has an unusual railway line that runs to Palma several times a day. The train is a narrow-gauge train and has antique mahogany and brass carriages. The railway station is based in what was once a 17th century manor house, which gives it a charming, oldie-world feel. Both Soller and Puerto de Soller have a traditional feel and atmosphere and it is very welcoming.

The journey between Palma and Soller by train passes through a specially-built tunnel in the mountains. As with the Soller tram, the views are breath-taking as you wind your way up through the mountains and lemon groves, an experience not to miss if you're visiting the area. Other attractions around Soller include a botanical garden, and a working finca Can Det Finca, which has a working traditional olive press. Both are open to the public. There are plenty of restaurants and bars in Soller, with some lovely traditional Mallorcan cuisine including, of course, fresh fish and seafood dishes. You'll also find more great restaurants down in Puerto de Soller, especially around the harbour area…

Soller

Soller is approximately 35 km (about miles) from Palma de Mallorca airport, and the transfer journey, if travelling by car, takes around 45 minutes to an hour, via a winding mountain road. The road is very scenic with views stretching for miles around. Depending on the amount of luggage you have with you, and the time of day, the train from Palma could also be an option, giving you the opportunity to relax and take in the amazing views. What a way to arrive!

A taste of traditional Majorca, Soller is a walker's paradise and a great base for exploring the western part of the island…

Torrenova

Torrenova is a great destination for family beach holidays, set on a quiet headland overlooking the sparkling blue Mediterranean Sea, with all the action and nightlife of Magaluf just a short stroll away.

Torrenova is a small resort that blends almost seamlessly with its very close neighbours, Palma Nova and Magaluf…

Torrenova

Set on the headland of a peninsula in south west Majorca, Torrenova is the quieter of the three resorts, almost sandwiched between the other two, offering a haven for families and those who prefer to stay in a quieter spot, whilst having all the action of the livelier resorts right on the doorstep. The three resorts practically merge together and it isn't obvious where each one begins and ends, so it is easy to walk between them and you can take your pick of the beaches on either side.

Susie in the sea on holiday

This pretty spot attracts a great number of visitors each summer, many of whom return faithfully year after year, safe in the knowledge that they will have the perfect family holiday, in a friendly, safe setting with a friendly atmosphere. In particular, Torrenova is popular with British tourists and many British come here to run a small business or retire to in sunnier climes. The resort is surprisingly pretty, and its location on the headland makes it a sun trap, with the glorious sandy Son Matias beach of soft, sandy and safe. The beach has all the amenities you would expect from a purpose built holiday resort, including life guards and first aid posts, and there are plenty of sun loungers and parasols for hire…

Torrenova

Torrenova has plenty of facilities such as bars, restaurants and lots of shops line the attractive sea front area, with many British themed establishments offering full English and British food, as well as favourite beers from Britain and Ireland.

The resort's many restaurants are friendly and good value, serving everything from fresh local cuisine, fish dishes and seafood to international options and pub grub...

Torrenova

Torrenova is popular with British ex-pats and holiday makers alike and it is a home from home for British visitors and is one that they return to year after year.

There are plenty of shops selling all kinds of clothing and beachwear, inflatable's and toys, souvenirs and mementoes, and all the holiday essentials. So get your bucket and spade and head off to the beautiful sandy beach…

Torrenova

In Torrenova you can visit the local market on a Thursday and Saturday, for more bargains and a good selection of local produce.

There are plenty of general shops and supermarkets dotted around the streets, many selling international brands, often in demand by self-catering holiday makers. You can hire cars, bikes or mopeds for exploring the area a little further, including family bikes for a fun experience! This is a good base for fun-filled family holidays, close to water parks and golf courses, and with plenty of amusements and bouncy castles to keep little ones entertained. Clean and well-presented, the resort and its neighbours have everything you could need for families of all ages. Torrenova is about 15 km from Palma airport, with transfer time from the airport usually around 20-30 minutes. Torrenova is a pleasant resort, with a sandy beach and friendly atmosphere. The vibrant nightlife of Magaluf is just a short stroll away…

Valldemossa

Valldemossa is a relaxed, authentic Majorcan village packed with lots of character, set amidst breath-taking scenery of mountains and coastline and a must for all those who like a quieter lifestyle during their holiday..

Valldemossa is a secluded, quaint Majorcan village, tucked away in the heart of the stunning Serra Tramuntana mountain range in the north-west of the island…

Valldemossa

The village of Valldemossa is inland, about a mile from the west coast of the island, and offers spectacular views out over the sea.

Just 20 km from Palma airport, the village is a quiet and relaxed place with a small resident population, popular with holiday makers looking for a peaceful base for exploring the area…

Valldemossa

The area of Valldemossa attracts many walkers, climbers and cyclists, and many routes are directly accessible from Valldemossa. Relatively undiscovered as a holiday destination, Valldemossa is known to independent travellers for its beautiful setting amongst an area of spectacular natural beauty, with a backdrop of mountains and countryside all around. The village also attracts a great number of day-trippers who travel here by tour bus.

The village is charming and pretty, with cobbled narrow old streets that wind and twist surprisingly in all directions. There are a number of friendly cafes and restaurants where you can sample the delights of local cuisine and hospitality. The village also has plenty of ancient architecture that is of historical significance…

Valldemossa

In Valldemossa there is a monastery Sa Cartoxia, and an interesting church and palace Palau de rei Sanxo, which has been the subject of attacks from Pirates for many centuries.

Why not visit the Nee S'albufereta nature reserve (see above) for breath-taking countryside views, Valldemossa is an ideal base to explore Majorca's north-west. It is charming, relaxed and very friendly. Now that we have explored the island it is now time for us to head into the capital city of Palma de Mallorca for a cultural and shopping extravaganza…

Palma de Mallorca

Palma de Mallorca is the capital of the island of Majorca and a absolute must to visit for everyone who comes to the island on a holiday. We have had many two week summer holidays on the island and have visited Palma de Mallorca on several occassions per holiday. When you do you will be stepping into a world of stylish pavement cafes, chic boutique shops on winding streets: vibrant and sophisticated, Palma has cultural and architectural delights aplenty, a buzzing atmosphere and upbeat nightlife. The buildings, churches and the cathedral warrant a day site seeing on there own. This truly is the beautiful jewel in the Majorca crown.

Palma de Mallorca, or Palma, is Majorca's capital city and home to its airport, which is about 6 km east of the city itself…

Palma de Mallorca:

Palma de Mallorca is situated in the middle of the Bay of Palma in the south west of the island, Palma is a glittering city, packed with culture, style and sophistication.

Its architecture and ambience are breath-taking and there is so much to see and do in the city that you will never be bored…

Palma de Mallorca:

Palma de Mallorca is busy and cosmopolitan, beautiful yet often crowded and hectic, as tourists mingle with residents going about their day to day lives but there are always places to sit in the shade and watch the people go by.

There are plenty of narrow streets and squares or plazas, with an array of chic boutiques and galleries…

Palma de Mallorca:

The city is a shopper's delight and has a very fashionable array of shops offering designer clothing, jewellery and accessories. So if you like to shop until you drop then this is the place to spend some time in.

Palma is a fascinating place for people watching and there are plenty of stylish cafes and bars in which you can lounge for hours watching the crowds go by over a few coffees or beers or just admiring some of the great cacti that are on display in some of the cities flower beds…

Palma de Mallorca:

Palma de Mallorca is romantic and chic, with a wonderful atmosphere that has long attracted artists and musicians as well as the rich and famous. For dining, the city has a great number of excellent restaurants with plenty of traditional cuisine: tapas, seafood and fresh locally caught fish, rustic meat stews and lamb dishes. You will be spoiled for choice whatever you fancy to eat or drink in this vibrant city.

Nightlife is fairly frantic although less full-on than Majorca's party resorts. There are also many theatre and ballet shows in Palma, and the city hosts many festivals and exhibitions throughout the year. So there is something for all tastes in entertainment.

Palma is a far cry from the lively tourist resorts of Magaluf and El Arenal, the city is a chic and hip, and increasingly attracts city-break tourists and weekend visitors throughout the year. Palma has a great number of hotels, mainly at the luxury end of the market…

Palma de Mallorca:

Visitors to Palma de Mallorca are often attracted by the colourful history of Majorca's capital city. which is known to date back to Roman times, although many of the streets and features date from the 19th and 20th centuries as the city has been transformed, with many old Roman features sadly lost to development of roads over recent times.

The skyline of Palma de Mallorca is dominated by the stunning 14th century gothic Cathedral, La Seu, a must for any visitor to see, which overlooks the city and the glittering harbour, frequented by luxury yachts and cruise ships…

Palma de Mallorca:

In Palma de Mallorca the other notable tourist attractions around the city include Bellver Castle (featured below), Almudaina Palace and Banyas Arabs, famous Moorish baths dating from the 10th century.

When you have seen enough of the sites in the city you could go to the very small beach in Palma de Mallorca itself however it is only a short distance in either direction to find the lovely sandy beaches at Can Pastilla and Cala Mayor…

Palma de Mallorca:

Public transport in the city is good with various options and it is easy to take a bus from Palma de Mallorca to any of the surrounding resorts. The city of Palma de Mallorca has a resident population of around 300,000 (approximately half of the island of Majorca's total population).

Palma de Mallorca is a beautiful, sophisticated and charming city, with an array of galleries and boutiques, bars and restaurants. Chic and cultured, a perfect European city short break destination. So if you want somewhere exciting to visit in the autumn, winter, spring or summer months then this city is for you. After enjoying all the sites and shopping experiences in the city it is sadly time, in the last chapter, for us all to leave the paradise island of Majorca…

Leaving Majorca

We have been visiting Majorca from time to time for more than forty years for our summer holidays and we have never been disappointed.

Palma Airport

Over the years we have stayed in the resorts of Porto Colom, Magaluf, Pollensa, S'Illot and Sa Coma and also visited most of the villages and towns that are featured in this book…

Leaving Majorca:

Finally before we go here are a few views of Majorca…

Leaving Majorca:

Finally before we go here are a few more views of Majorca…

Leaving Majorca:

Susie and I always pack our suitcase with not just our swim wear, shorts and tee-shirts but flip-flops, sunglasses, sun hats and sun cream. We also take our own kettle so we can have a cup of tea or coffee on our holiday balcony at anytime we want. As we leave Majorca I hope that when you are planning your next Mediterranean holiday you will consider Majorca as a place that could be for you.

So as we fly off into the sun and leave the beautiful island of Majorca behind I would like to thank you for your company and wish you a **Great and HAPPY HOLIDAY in the Future** wherever you choose to go…

Acknowledgement

I would like to acknowledge and thank ALL the people of Majorca who have made all of our family holidays to their beautiful island over the years such a positive and happy experience for us. A special mention and thank you must go to all the local Spanish people who keep every resort and beach spotlessly clean at all times.

Thank You and Well Done

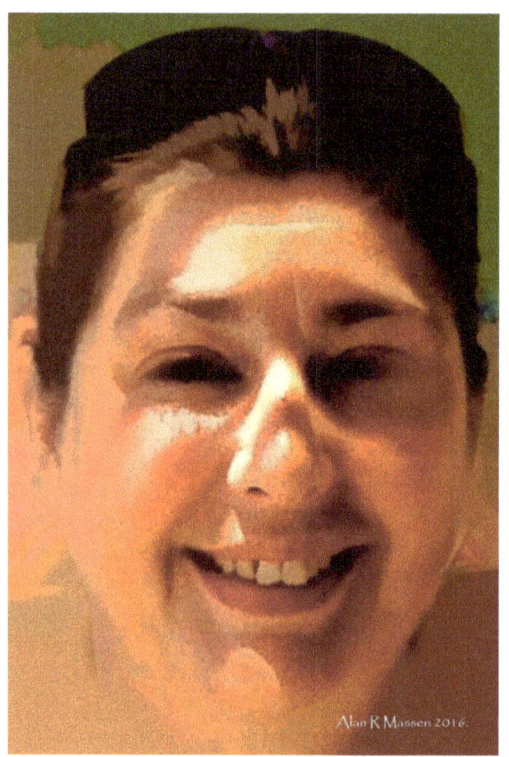 

Susie and Alan on one of their holidays

Finally, for me, I believe that the most important thing to ensure that you enjoy your holiday to the full is that you have someone to share your experiences with you. I am lucky I have my wife Susie as my companion on our Mediterranean and UK holidays. Her smile and enthusiasm makes every day of our stays abroad and at home very happy and memorable for me. Thank you my love…

Copyright © 2019 Alan R. Massen

www.ingramcontent.com/pod-product-compliance
Lightning Source LLC
Chambersburg PA
CBHW061927290426
44113CB00024B/2835